FRAGMENTED CATALONIA

About Policy Network

Policy Network is an international thinktank and research institute. Its network spans national borders across Europe and the wider world with the aim of promoting the best progressive thinking on the major social and economic challenges of the 21st century.

Our work is driven by a network of politicians, policymakers, business leaders, public service professionals, and academic researchers who work on long-term issues relating to public policy, political economy, social attitudes, governance and international affairs. This is complemented by the expertise and research excellence of Policy Network's international team.

A platform for research and ideas

- Promoting expert ideas and political analysis on the key economic, social and political challenges of our age.
- Disseminating research excellence and relevant knowledge to a wider public audience through interactive policy networks, including interdisciplinary and scholarly collaboration.
- Engaging and informing the public debate about the future of European and global progressive politics.

A network of leaders, policymakers and thinkers

- Building international policy communities comprising individuals and affiliate institutions.
- Providing meeting platforms where the politically active, and potential leaders of the future, can engage with each other across national borders and with the best thinkers who are sympathetic to their broad aims.
- Engaging in external collaboration with partners including higher education institutions, the private sector, thinktanks, charities, community organisations, and trade unions.
- Delivering an innovative events programme combining in-house seminars with large-scale public conferences designed to influence and contribute to key public debates.

www.policy-network.net

FRAGMENTED CATALONIA

Divisive legacies of a push for secession

Adolf Tobeña

policy network

ROWMAN &
LITTLEFIELD
———— INTERNATIONAL

London • New York

4501 Forbes Boulevard, Suite 200, Lanham, Maryland 20706, USA
With additional offices in Boulder, New York, Toronto (Canada), and Plymouth (UK)
www.rowman.com

Copyright © 2021, Adolf Tobeña

All rights reserved. No part of this book may be reproduced in any form or by any electronic or mechanical means, including information storage and retrieval systems, without written permission from the publisher, except by a reviewer who may quote passages in a review.

British Library Cataloguing in Publication Data
A catalogue record for this book is available from the British Library

ISBN: PB 978-1-53814-736-8

Library of Congress Cataloging-in-Publication Data

Names: Tobeña, Adolf, 1950- author.
Title: Fragmented Catalonia : divisive legacies of a push for secession / Adolf Tobeña.
Description: Lanham, Maryland : Policy Network/Rowman & Littlefield International, 2021. | Includes bibliographical references. | Summary: "The Catalonian secessionist crisis was the most noticeable event that Spain offered to Western politics in the opening decades of this century. Within this time – characterised as it is by huge technological acceleration, myriad online and trade interactions across multiple levels, high levels of political polarisation, and widespread feelings of collective unease and discontent – the Catalonian secessionist movement has become one of the prevalent topics of public policy and political debate in the European Union. The Catalonian matter is often reduced to a narrative that Catalonian citizens – typically dynamic, engaging and with the wonderful city of Barcelona as their capital – are not at ease with life within Spain and would like to rule their society and to organise their lives themselves. Meanwhile, the central authority in Spain resists any demand for attaining sovereignty. This antagonism has poisoned the relations between regional and central authorities and the conviviality among many Catalonian citizens. This paper explores the existence of other Catalonian citizens who do not usually appear in tellings of this often truncated and over-simplified story. There is great diversity within this group, CatSpanish, a citizenry which recognises and declares a double national identity – both Catalonian and Spanish, to varying degrees for each person – in terms of feelings of belonging"—Provided by publisher.
Identifiers: LCCN 2021014391 (print) | LCCN 2021014392 (ebook) | ISBN 9781538147368 (paperback) | ISBN 9781538147375 (epub)
Subjects: LCSH: Citizenship—Spain—Catalonia. | National characteristics, Catalan. | National characteristics, Spanish. | Decentralization in government—Spain. | Migration, Internal—Social aspects.—Spain. | Catalonia (Spain)—History—Autonomy and independence movements. | Catalonia (Spain)—Social conditions—21st century.
Classification: LCC JN8399.C2665 T63 2021 (print) | LCC JN8399.C2665 (ebook) | DDC 946.7083—dc23
LC record available at https://lccn.loc.gov/2021014391
LC ebook record available at https://lccn.loc.gov/2021014392

CONTENTS

Preface	vii
Acknowledgements	xiii
Situation Maps	1
CatSpanish Citizenry: From Silence to Prominence	13
The Void of the Central Spanish State	19
Secessionist Top Leaders	25
Madrid-Barcelona Competition	31
Dual Identities: "As Catalan as Spanish"	41
Cantonalism and Cainism in Spain	49
Longitudinal Profiles of Catalonian Citizenry	55
Immersive Education: Another Divisive Tool	81
A Dangerous Decade (2010-2020)	101
CatSpanish Melancholy: Temptative Prescriptions	107
Epilogue	115
Postscript	119

Postscript II	125
References	135
Notes	145
About the Author	151

Regarding Images

Readers are advised to go to Tobeña, A (2021) "Fragmented Catalonia", Policy Network paper (https://policynetwork.org/publications/papers/fragmented-catalonia/) for a better reading of some of the Figures as they appear in full colour and proper sizes.

PREFACE

The Catalonian secessionist crisis was the most noticeable event that Spain offered to Western politics in the opening decades of this century. Within this time, characterised as it is by huge technological acceleration, myriad online and trade interactions across multiple levels, high levels of political polarisation, and widespread feelings of collective unease and discontent, the Catalonian secessionist movement has become one of the prevalent topics of public policy and political debate in the European Union (EU).

The secessionist movement in Catalonia coincided with the double fragmentary shock that affected another European polity, given the tortuous and protracted Brexit process and with the related increasing drive towards Scottish independence being experienced in the United Kingdom (UK). Each of these movements—Catalan secession, Scottish independence, and the UK's withdrawal from the EU—continue to play out and continue to arouse curiosity. It does this given the initial outbreak, gradual growth, remarkable staying-power, and the subsequent entrenchment of positions in each case that resulted from these different secessionist movements, each of them experiments uniquely European in nature.

A number of characteristic and overlapping ingredients have defined the Catalonian secessionist bid, including:

1. The movement crystallized through enormous and frequent street demonstrations which displayed an enormous mobilising capacity and a highly effective and sustained form of activism;
2. The apparently grassroots movement had a firm direction exercised by the regional government and the autonomous parliament. Both behaved in blatant violation of constitutional and home rule norms through iterated and defiant disobedient acts;
3. Media outlets under the direct (or indirect) control of the region's autonomous administration have expressed an uninhibited and systematic bias in favour of secession;
4. The movement asserted its influence partly through the presence, often overwhelmingly so, of secessionist symbols and emblems in many aspects of public life, including with flags, banners and billboards in many public places;
5. The secessionist bid was pursued in the absence of any clear social majority in favour of independence in the region;
6. There was a highly effective silencing of non-secessionist public opinion throughout much of the enduring secessionist campaign and subsequent litigation;
7. A curious paralysis was induced, which later evolved into irritation, confusion and anguish, at the level of the Spanish central administration and, with it, among many within the wider Spanish population who followed the course of the conflict with a mix of perplexity, fatigue and boredom;
8. Deep divisions appeared and became entrenched and often highly confrontational between the two main segments of the Catalonian population—that is, between secessionists and unionists[1]; and
9. All this happened in one of the richest and most advanced regions of Southern Europe within a tolerant and fully open democratic context.

Those distinctive features are also behind the frequent scrutiny that the secessionist crisis has received from some of the most followed and prestigious tribunes of international journalism. And from this, too, comes the prominence of Catalonian political leaders and celebrities in visible positions throughout Spanish and European societies. Few can ignore this lively corner of the western Mediterranean, much loved as a destination for tourists and lovers of culture, whose capital Barcelona is consistently ranked among Europe's favourite cities, and that plays host to one of the most well-known and internationally followed soccer teams in the world, Barça FC.

In much international media coverage, the Catalonian matter is often reduced to the following: Catalonian citizens, typically so dynamic and engaging, with such a wonderful city, Barcelona, as their capital, and who have created that fantastic toy for global entertainment, Barça FC, are not at ease with life within Spain and would like to rule their society and to organise their lives themselves. Meanwhile, the central authority in Spain resists any demand for attaining sovereignty, which brings to the fore the country's latent authoritarianism by not even allowing the region to settle the issue, in a civilized way, by authorising a referendum—contrary, it should be said, to what has happened in Scotland, given the 2014 independence referendum which confirmed Scotland's place within the UK, at least for now. Spain has even gone so far as to imprison several Catalonian leaders who organised unauthorised and illegal consultations to gauge the opinion of the citizenry about the prospect of seceding from Spain. This antagonism and conflict has poisoned the relations between regional and central authorities and the conviviality among many Catalonian citizens.

This book will provide a report into the existence of other Catalonian citizens who do not usually appear in tellings of this often truncated and over-simplified story. There is great diversity within this group, which I deign to call *CatSpanish* for simplicity, and because this denomination fits in many cases with their identifiable characteristics, as we will see later. In short, the *CatSpanish* citizenry recognise and declare a double national identity—both Catalonian and Spanish, to varying degrees for each person—in terms of feelings of belonging. However, I do not seek to provide a complete definition for this cohort, as to do so would be impossible within these pages, but I will provide a broad-brush account of this diverse majoritarian group throughout the book. This is because, firstly, I am aware that such definitions of habits, attitudes and behaviours are always simplifications, and secondly, as above, because any full characterisation would require an in depth and extremely fine-grained analysis that is beyond the scope of this analysis.

The tense and embittered dispute between Catalonian citizens who are in favour of segregation from Spain and those who prefer to maintain the ties that unite them to the rest of Spain, has, to a large extent, poisoned the good governance and the enjoyment of the undeniable amenities of the region. It should be noted that a portion of *CatSpanish citizens* would also like to be rid of the burdens of Spanish rule, but that is not a crucial defining feature of this cohort, as there are quite a few in the rest of Spain who would also appreciate being liberated from Spanish rule. Therefore, it is not necessary to automatically equate *CatSpanish* citizenry with those who favour unionism with Spain: the matter is much more intricate and as I progress by sketching and analysing a wide range of relevant data, hopefully I will shed some light on this complex group.

The core political attribute that defines individuals as *CatSpanish* is that they identify, often intimately, with the air, the environment and the multitude of ingredients and variants that makes up the great bounty of Spanish traditions. In other words, they relate to the rich tapestry of the peoples who have made the Iberian Peninsula their home throughout the centuries. In Catalonia there are many such people—in fact, they are probably the majority.

The first two chapters present a brief portrait of the place of Catalonia within Spain and the main political events and recent electoral results that underpin the entrenched and polarised situation that has taken room in the region in the wake of the secession push. Chapters 3 and 4 present several profiles of political leaders and prominent celebrities from both the secessionist and unionist fields. Chapter 5 presents an attempt to characterise the permanent competition between the main economic and cultural poles within contemporary Spain—Barcelona vs Madrid—and the crucial impact this has on Spanish politics. Chapter 6 summarises the key identity traits and essential characteristics that define the majoritarian segment of the Catalonian citizenry, namely, those that treasure dual national identities, feeling both Catalan and Spanish. Chapter 7 describes the current iteration of the tradition of fierce factionalism within Spanish politics. Chapter 8 provides the core of the essay and presents in detail the longitudinal findings that allow for the characterisation of the main vectors which lead to the current political and social fracturing of Catalonian society through a distinctive ethnolinguistic cleavage. The linguistic and economic segmentations through which the division has occurred are described using data from across two decades. The fissure came, in essence, as a result of concerted action involving a proudly disloyal regional government and a network of local elites and activist organisations, that worked to promote a secessionist agenda that is against the wishes of more than half of the Catalonian population. The crucial role played by regional media outlets is also analysed here. Chapter 9 contains a description of the most valuable data that has been accrued on the Catalonian educational system, which has also proven to be a powerful tool to promote division within society. Chapters 10 and 11 offer additional perspectives to try to help readers to better understand the seriousness of the division within Catalonia and the reverberations and polarising effects this has induced in Spain's politics. In the epilogue and postscript, I try, finally, to summarise the current political stalemate given the paralyzing shock of the Covid-19 pandemic.

This essay was initially conceived as an expansion of a paper by Josep M Oller JM, Albert Satorra and Adolf Tobeña entitled *'Pathways and legacies of the secessionist push in Catalonia: linguistic frontiers, economic segments and media roles within a divided society'* that was published by *Policy Network* in October 2019 and is available here.[2]

The final form of the book derives from a series of research studies that describe the evolution of the main vectors through which the deep fissure in Catalonian society was created, as a result of a top-down planned and openly announced attempt at secession that was commanded by a partisan autonomous administration that had convinced less than half of Catalonians to support them. These findings come from a joint and very fruitful research endeavour that I shared with my colleagues Josep M. Oller (University of Barcelona) and Albert Satorra (Universitat Pompeu Fabra, Barcelona). They are described, in detail, at several papers in specialised journals (87, 88, 89, 90, 91, 92). The book covers a wider range of areas and enters into the profiling of prominent social figures and chronicles more deeply some of the circumstances and events that may help to define this entrenched political crisis.

ACKNOWLEDGEMENTS

This essay derived from a series of collaborative research projects launched with my colleagues Josep María Oller (University of Barcelona, UB) and Albert Satorra (Pompeu Fabra University, UPF Barcelona), in early 2018. In 2019, we published *Pathways and legacies of the secessionist push in Catalonia: linguistic frontiers, economic segments and media roles within a divided society*, Policy Network Paper, October, (https://policynetwork.org/publications/papers/pathways-and-legacies-of-the-secessionist-push-in-catalonia/). That online essay was the frontispiece for a series of research papers by those three authors that characterized the evolution of Catalonian secession bid from 2006-2020. The bulk of this research appears, summarized, at chapter 8 of this book.

As we were analysing details of the statistical series that permitted an exhaustive characterisation of the main vectors behind the secession bid in Catalonia, I enjoyed the enormous privilege to be guided by two distinguished statisticians who treasure a deep knowledge of their field and a devotion for precision and restraint. Our discussions at the UPF campus or over coffees in downtown Barcelona were often a refuge of fruitful symbiosis and lively friendship. Two of the chapters of this book (chapter 1: Situation maps; chapter 8: Longitudinal profiles of Catalonian citizenry) are the result of common and intensive work over two years and they ought to be reported as written by three Authors. The rest of this essay also owns a big debt to them as it was enriched by their illuminating comments.

Barry Colfer from Policy Network guided us first on the inaugural paper of the series of research studies that form the crucial backbone of this essay, and afterwards stimulated and primed us to write a short essay on the topic of "Fragmented Catalonia" (his title for the book, by the way). I took the job of finishing it and he has accompanied me through all stages of writing with dedication and great care. Josh Newlove, from Policy Network, also provided all kinds of help Dhara Snowden and Rebecca Anastasi at Rowman and Littlefield also deserve praise for a fine and meticulous job of producing the final book.

London-based Spanish friends gave support to this endeavour and skilfully moved all kind of resources that allowed us to secure the necessary funds for this publication.

Damián Gil M.D., provided the first script that permitted me access to build the database of the full series of CEO Barometers. OEC Group members (Barcelona) provided lively discussions with suggestions that improved and helped to focus and refine the research that informs this essay.

It is compulsory to refer to the excellent disposition of Policy Network, Palgrave Communications, Genealogy, The Economic Journal, Fundación Europea Sociedad y Educación, and the European Journal of Language Policy, to permit the adaptation of figures and tables that appeared, in previous versions, in these different sources. EDLibros-Barcelona was eager to allow me to adapt several texts for this essay that had appeared, in Spanish language, at Tobeña A (2020) "Catañoles", EDLibros, Barcelona. It is also necessary to acknowledge the debt I owe to "El País", "El Español" and Catarata Ed, for reproducing several fragments of texts which are duly referenced here. I am also grateful to the graph files of "La Vanguardia".

CEO-Catalunya and CIS-Spain, provide a rich and open source of sociological data with splendid and commendable regularity.

ACKNOWLEDGEMENTS

GESOP-Barcelona and Metroscopia-Madrid also deserve acknowledgement for adapting some of their published data.

Finally, my work on this essay was partially supported by AFOSR-MINERVA FA9550-18-0496 Grant (as an ARTIS International Senior Fellow: https://artisinternational.org/) and Bial Foundation Grant 163/14.

SITUATION MAPS

ANTECEDENTS

Catalonia is one of the seventeen autonomous regions that comprise contemporary Spain (Figure 1.1). The region is politically designated as a ***nationality*** by its Statute of Autonomy, and the regional government and autonomous parliament make the rules relating to most issues relating to citizen's lives and occupations as a result of the wide-ranging executive, legislative and fiscal responsibilities and capabilities that it enjoys. Catalonia capital city, Barcelona, is the second largest in Spain, after Madrid, and is the centre of one the largest metropolitan areas in the Mediterranean basin.

Spanish Catalonia comprises most of the territory of a medieval Principality that was part of the Aragon Kingdom that joined the Castilian Kingdom to form modern Spain in the fifteenth century. A minor part of Catalonia, on the Northern side of the Pyrenees mountains remained under French rule and is currently a small French "*department*" with Perpignan as its capital.

The current population of Catalonia is around 7,500,000 citizens: 42–45 percent can be described as being of 'native ascendancy' or have long ago assimilated, and the remaining 55-58 percent settled in the region during the twentieth century, arriving within several

Figure 1.1 Spain's regions.

migratory waves from the rest of Spain and more recently from many other origins.

The official languages in Catalonia are Catalan, Spanish and Aranese (a variant of the Occitan language). According to the most recent survey of common linguistic uses in the region (Idescat2018[1]), the habitual languages of the citizenry is Spanish (56 percent); Catalan (36 percent); both Spanish and Catalan languages (6 percent); and other languages (5 percent), including: Arab, Italian, Urdu, Romanian, English, Chinese, French and the Amazigh (Berber) languages.

A BRIEF ON CATALONIAN SECESSION PUSH.

The enduring secessionist challenge in Catalonia has dominated Spain's political landscape in recent years, creating a stalemate that shows no signs of disappearing. Over the last decade, secessionist forces won four regional elections and were able to sustain governments by tiny majorities in the region's autonomous parliament. Two illegal consultations regarding self-determination were called during this period, and around 2 million (38 percent of Catalonia's eligible voters) supported secession from Spain. Following the second consultation on 1 October 2017, an "Independence Declaration" was officially proclaimed by the autonomous parliament on 27 October 2017, an action which was instantly followed by the suspension of home rule for the region, as sanctioned by the Spanish Parliament, that endured until mid-2018.

The secessionist parties reasserted their lead at the regional elections on 27 December 2017. These elections were called by the Spanish government as a way to try to solve the constitutional logjam that the independence declaration had created and to put an end to the suspension of home rule that had been put in place two months previously. The results, however, merely confirmed the stagnation although the formation of a new regional government had to wait until mid-2018, after several unsuccessful attempts by the leaders of the independence movement to reinstate a government while several of them were in prison or had fled into exile. These strenuous efforts to form a government were all blocked by legal provisions dictated by the Spanish High Court.

A left-wing government was formed in Spain in June 2018 led by the centre-left *Partido Socialista Obrero Español* (PSOE)[2] which initially had the support of the Catalonian and Basque nationalist parties. This new scenario seemed to open up opportunities to explore plausible solutions for the chronically entrenched situation. However, exploratory talks between the Spanish government and the new secessionist Catalan government did not lead to substantial progress. At Spain's general election on the 28 April 2019, left-wing parties strengthened their lead in the parliament in Madrid without reaching a stable majority and the formation of a new social democratic/left populist government had to wait until January 2020, after another general election was held on 10 November 2019. The final sentencing of the rebellious secessionist leaders by the Supreme

Court[3] was handed down on 10 October 2019, which condemned several of the secessionist leaders to several years in prison for sedition, and also for embezzlement.

The main social consequence of the secessionist campaign has been the build-up of a deep political divide between two large segments of Catalonian citizenry, between *unionists and secessionists*, which was absent before the surge in support for segregation from Spain. The lack of a majority behind the vigorous, perseverant but failed secessionist venture injected friction and tension into Catalan society that was hitherto largely unknown (3, 4, 17, 25, 26, 39, 123). Close neighbours, colleagues, acquaintances and even friends and families who had different feelings of identification with Catalonia and Spain (to varying degrees for each person), as part of their intimate identities, attachments and values, became sharply divided on the issue of secession and must now continue to live together amid this unsolved tension.

Distinctions around one's "*sense of belonging*" (*national identity feelings*) can be used as a good indicator of the divide that exists between secessionists and unionists (89, 90, 91, 92). Secessionists tend to declare an almost exclusive affective attachment to Catalonia, whereas unionists display various communal bonds, with a dominant sense of attachment to both Spain and Catalonia (i.e. *Catspanish*). This gap between these two predominant forms of national identification in Catalonia is rather recent and appeared largely as a consequence of the abrupt polarization on the issue of secession in recent years. The accentuation of affective features of identity around a specific political divide (i.e. accept/reject secession, in this case), reproduce similar paths towards increasing animosity and ruthless partisanship that has characterized recent political struggle in several Western societies (127, 129). The harsh partisanship that now exists between many democrats and republicans in the US that grew through an increasingly narrow fusion of self and group identities is a prominent example of this (21, 73, 74), as is the contemptuous struggle that divided the UK population on the issue of remaining or leaving the EU (49, 57, 129, 130).

FROM ABRUPT POLARISATION TO CHRONIC ENTRENCHMENT

By way of illustration, it is convenient to start by depicting the preferences of Catalonian citizens on the issue of secession throughout the period that is analysed in this essay, namely between 2006–2020. Figure 1 shows the evolution of public opinion regarding the question of secession based on representative samples of Catalan citizenry through successive opinion polls undertaken by the *Centre d'Estudis d'Opinió* (CEO)—the polling agency of the Catalonian regional government—during this period.

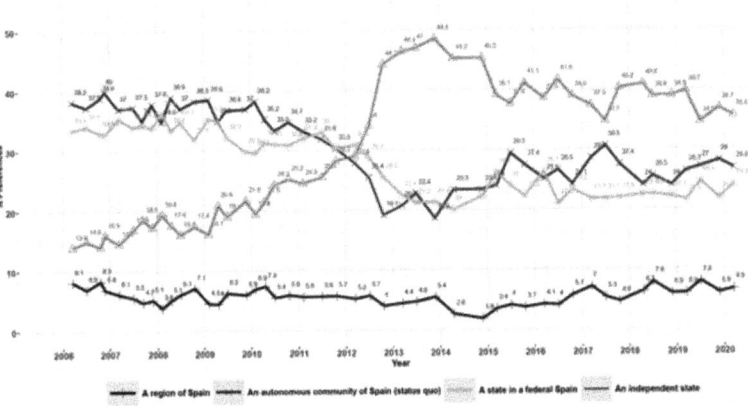

Figure 1.2 **Preferences of Catalan citizens (in percentages) regarding the political status of the region.** The political organisation of Spain is in many aspects federal and highly decentralised. Regions with home rule powers are referred to as "autonomous communities" rather than "states" for historical reasons. The perception of coincidence is illustrated by the two lines of the graph following an almost identical course throughout subsequent CEO surveys (see CEO Barometer of Political Opinion, available here.[4] Data was gathered from personal interviews with representative samples of 1500-2500 citizens for each survey (the most recent iteration depicted in Figure 2 took place on 31 July 2020). 'Autonomous community' thus best describes the current status of Catalonia within Spain, which denotes a highly decentralised region with powers of home rule. The proportion of DK/NA (do not know or no answers) are omitted.

This series of polls were initiated in 2006. Preferences on the status of the region showed a fairly stable pattern until 2010, at which point the secessionist segment started to gradually increase over two years, which was followed by an abrupt eruption from October 2012 peaking around the start of 2014. In numbers, in January 2010, those who wanted secession were below 20 percent; in October 2011, this had grown to 30 percent and since October 2012 this cohort stood above 45 percent, which provided the trigger for the secessionist breakaway. December 2014 marked the start of a small decline in support for secession that stabilised at about 40 percent of those surveyed, with minor oscillations. Figure 1.3 shows how, in raw percentages, those who supported remaining a part of Spain (in its various forms) and those supporting secession have been essentially tied since December 2014 which underscores the entrenched nature of the political divide. These results have been repeatedly confirmed, using different variations and methodologies, in surveys conducted by the Centro de Investigaciones Sociológicas (CIS), the survey agency of the Spanish government.[5]

The main consequence of the long secessionist campaign has been the creation of a deep division between secessionists and unionists—the two biggest segments of Catalonian citizens—a division that did

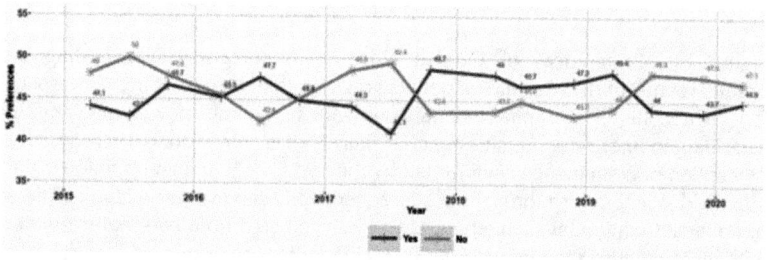

Figure 1.3 **Percentages of citizens responding YES/NO to a direct question about secession from Spain in a hypothetical referendum on self-determination.** CEO surveys, Barometer of Political Opinion, available here.[6] The proportion of 'DK/NA' are omitted.

not exist before the emergence of the secessionist movement. (3, 4, 17, 25, 26, 39, 122, 123)

This fragmentation also appears in the region's election results. Figures 1.4 and 1.5 illustrate the distinctive geographical distribution of secessionism and unionism in the results of the Catalan

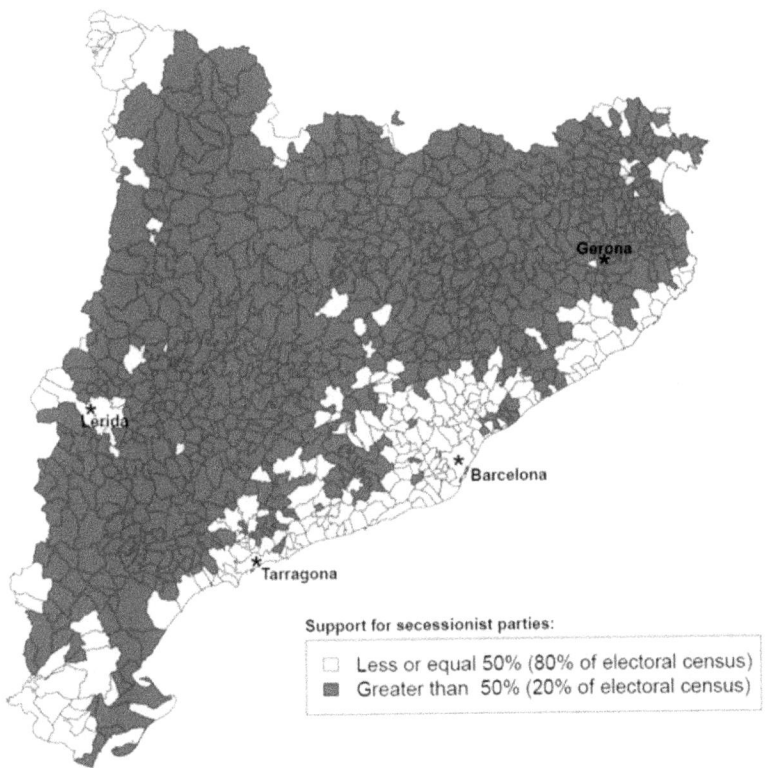

Figure 1.4 Geographic distribution of support for secessionist parties in the regional elections of 21 December 2017. *Source*: Official election data. Secessionist parties enjoy majority support in 76 per cent of municipalities, representing some 78 per cent of the total surface of the region, but only 20 per cent of the population, while the remaining 80 per cent of the population live in the remaining 24 per cent of municipalities where secessionist did not enjoy majority support. Thus, secessionism is highly concentrated in inland counties, whereas unionism predominates in the more populated coastal areas but also in some Pyrenean and peripheral counties as well.

regional elections in December 2017. Notably, secessionism dominates the vast and relatively less populated interior of the Catalan territory, while unionism prevails, although not so overwhelmingly, in the coastal conurbations.

Figure 1.4 can be complemented with details of total numbers (Table 1.1), derived from the electoral data from the 21 December 2017 regional elections.

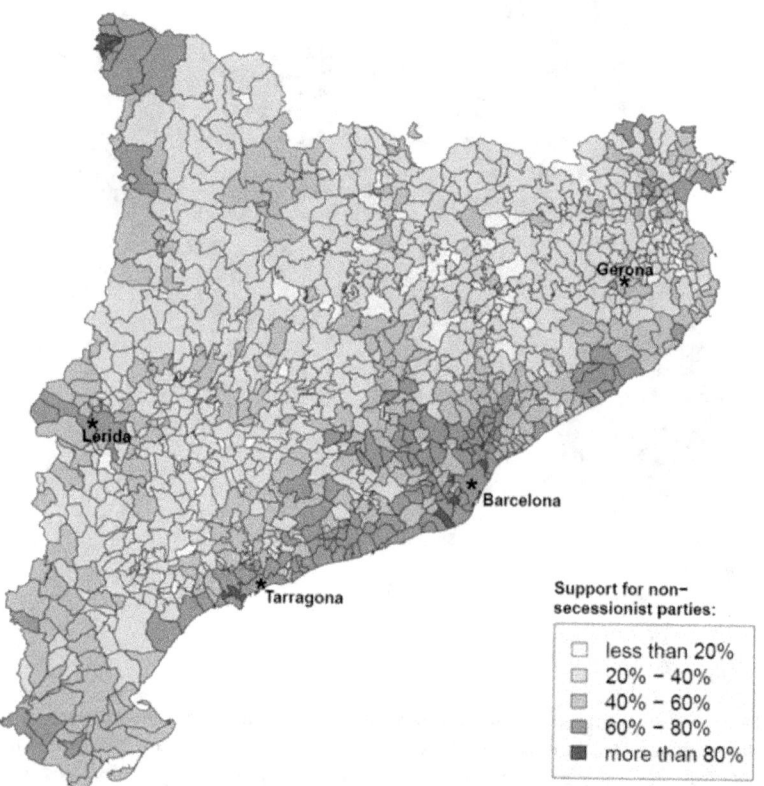

Figure 1.5 Percentage of unionist votes for non-secessionist parties at the 2017 regional elections, 21 December 2017. *Source*: Official election data. Unionism predominates in more populated coastal areas and in some Pyrenean and peripheral counties. Darker aeas denote higher support to the unionist formations as indicated by the scale set out above.

SITUATION MAPS

Table 1.1 Absolute potential support for secessionist and non-secessionist parties in the different geographic areas in the 2017 regional elections as set out in Figure 1.4; M = 1 million voters

	Secessionists	Non-Secessionists
Zone in Black	1.069M	0.434M
Zone in White	0.996M	2.829M
Total	2.065M	3.263M

In the two most recent regional contests, the difference in total votes for each sides was limited to a narrow margin of about 150,000 votes, with a unionist predominance on both occasions. Postscript II (p.125) contains a depiction of results of the last regional elections (14th February 2021). The gap of around 100,000 votes between unionist and secessionist forces persisted again. This time with secessionist votes on top, but with lowest turnout in history. The geographical distinctive distribution of pro-unionist and pro-secessionist forces depicted at Figure 1.4 and 1.5 also persisted unmodified. These maps therefore delimit, albeit only roughly, the distinctive geographical distribution of secessionist and unionist majorities.

In terms of linguistic identification, places with a clear predominance of native Catalan speakers on the one hand tend to have majority support for secession, and places with a clear predominance of native Spanish speakers or mixed speakers—or mostly *CatSpanish* areas, as I dub them in this essay—tend to have a majority that prefer to remain a part of Spain. This stark territorial distribution of political preferences relating to secession has been analysed as an ingredient anchored in the ancestry and family origin of citizens (1, 75, 104). In other words, as a segmentation that reflects the preponderance of native family origin, especially in the vast interior of the region, as opposed to the communities that built up as a result of successive migrations throughout especially the twentieth century in the more populated coastal areas. Thus, this political segmentation reflects a recognisable geographic, linguistic and socioeconomic stratification (for more on this, see chapter 8).

This geographical compartmentalisation of the secessionist and unionist votes also occurred, in a similar way, at the latest state-wide elections (see Figure 1.6). The results of this election marked a remarkable degree of similarity with the results of the 2017 regional elections that ended the differential trends in voting and abstention rates which had distinguished these types of elections from one another for decades. The polarisation around secession has been so intense that the electorate has ended up responding in much the same way regardless of the nature and subject of successive elections.

Finally, it should be reiterated that the absence of a clear majority behind the secessionist push opened up frictions and tensions between these two large population segments within Catalan society that were hitherto largely unknown until recent years (4, 10, 39, 61). As remarked previously neighbours, colleagues, acquaintances and even friends and families who had different feelings of belonging to and identification with Catalonia and Spain (to varying degrees for every person), became deeply divided on the issue of secession and must now continue to live together amid this unsolved and entrenched tension (26, 117, 118).

For years during the mounting and burgeoning secessionist campaign, the most common way to avoid this daily tension was simply to ignore it. But any attempt to bury the question did not help and has not resolved the underlying frictions. Almost everyone now recognizes the depth of the divide and many dare to comment on it without apprehension or inhibition. In this spirit, I have decided to undertake this preliminary tour of the *CatSpanish* universe.

SITUATION MAPS

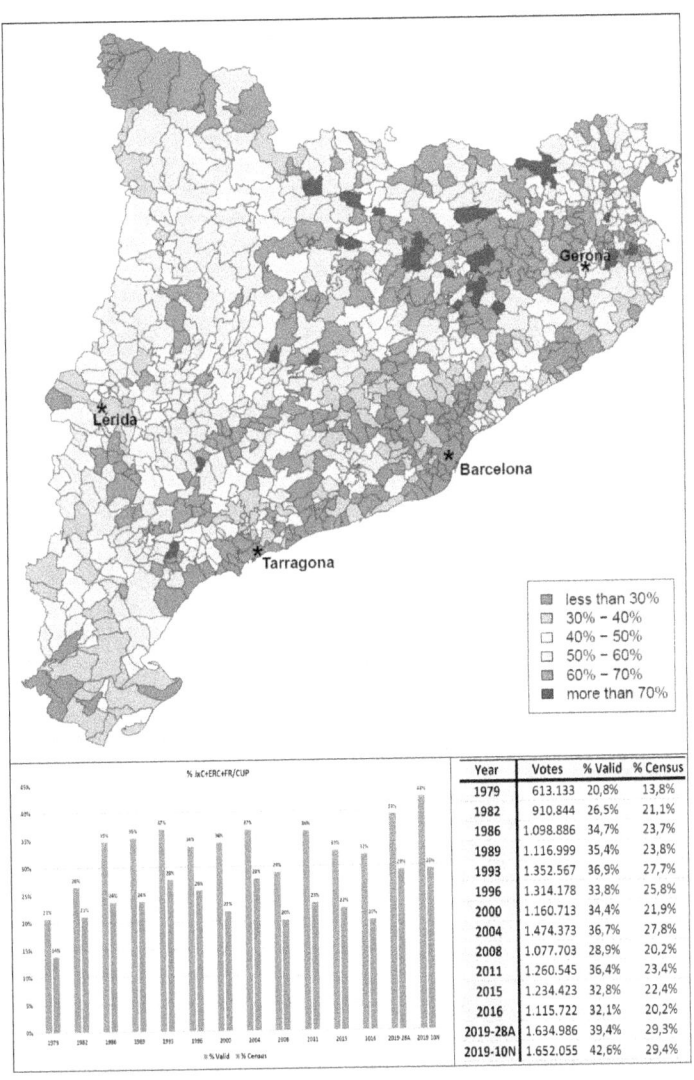

Figure 1.6 Territorial distribution of support for secessionist formations at the Spanish general election on 10 November 2019. Above Map: Geographical distribution of electoral support obtained by secessionist formations across Catalonia at the Spanish general election on 10 November 2019. Darker tones at the map indicated less support for secessionist forces. Below, left: Evolution of the totalper cent of votes obtained by the three main secessionist parties: JxCat, ERC and CUP[7]. Below, right: Absolute number of votes and percentages over total votes and all eligible voters (i.e. electoral census). *Source*: adapted from BREU de GESOP-43: Les eleccions generals del 10N: resultats a Catalunya[8].

CATSPANISH CITIZENRY
From Silence to Prominence

> *"I'm not abandoning Machado, or leaving Cervantes, or renouncing Rosalía".*
>
> Gabriel Rufián, in a speech to the Spanish Parliament during the session that approved the new central government in January 2020.

The secessionist push in Catalonia was strongly associated with a number of prominence of individuals who were born or are living in this North Eastern corner of the Iberian Peninsula, at the point where the Pyrenees encounter the Mediterranean. Never before in the ancient history of the diverse Spanish counties and communities has such a group of Catalonian figures been in the political and social limelight in Spain. Indeed, a good portion of the most high-profile characters on the Iberian cultural, social and political scene are dominated by noteworthy Catalonians, and no small amount of them are *CatSpanish*.

Today, the two most visible *CatSpanish* individuals on the domestic political scene are Inés Arrimadas and Gabriel Rufián (pictured below). Nowadays they are both at the very pinnacle of political life in Catalonia and across Spain. Arrimadas is among the most personable, charismatic and lively female voices that can be heard in the

Spanish Parliament. Rufián on the other hand is among the most forward, macho, and comedic characters who has spoken in the Palace of Carrera de San Jerónimo (the Spanish Parliament) in recent years.

Both Arrimadas and Rufián now serve in the national parliament in Madrid, after their respective rapid rise to stardom at the regional level in Barcelona. Both share youth and have come to be seen as aspiring leaders in the complex jungle of Catalan politics, having emerged as the secessionist conflict has played out. What's more, both embody, better than anyone else, the depth of the internal divide that has become so deeply entrenched within Catalonia.

Inés Arrimadas has been a persistent and forceful spokesperson for the unionist resistance throughout the secessionist campaign. Rufián, meanwhile, has represented the coolest face of the secessionist push through a range of established outlets in Barcelona, Madrid and further afield. While solid data is lacking, I would not be surprised if these two figures represent the two most divisive characters for their respective opponents.

Figure 2.1 Left: Inés Arrimadas, current leader of the "Ciudadanos (Citizens)" party, (since early 2020) the main centrist-liberal party in Spain, and chief of the opposition in the regional parliament in Catalonia from 2017-2019. Right: Gabriel Rufián, leader of ERC group (Esquerra Republicana de Catalunya) in the Spanish Parliament and one of the most prominent secessionist leaders.

Arrimadas now leads, with an effort worthy of a better cause, the tiny and greatly diminished liberal movement that remains in the Spanish parliament following the disastrous November 2019 election under the leadership of Albert Rivera—her leader and mentor within the *"Ciudadanos"* party—which saw the party shed 80 percent of its seats in parliament. Rivera was another ambitious *CatSpanish* figure, who was viewed by many as coming very close to reaching the helm of power in Spain, or at least an important post at the highest level of the Spanish government, before the 2019 electoral disaster.

Rufián, for his part, is now one of the main pillars of the central government in Madrid, since the parliamentary arithmetic makes the support of his ERC[1] grouping to allow the PSOE leadership to cling to power. Naturally this has granted him a key role in the national legislature since January 2020. Rufián has taken to this role naturally and seems fully at ease with this position at the very heart of Spanish politics. Still only in his 30s, much is expected from Rufián, and his communication and leadership gifts are widely acknowledged.

Today, Arrimadas clearly has a much more difficult job, at least politically speaking.[2] She became the main voice for the unionist community in Catalonia by winning, defying all serious forecasts, the regional elections of December 2017, after the failed secession attempt that autumn when large segments of the *CatSpanish* people placed their faith in her and in her party to counteract the dominance of the secessionist forces both on the streets and within the autonomous administration. In this election, the bulk of the citizenry in the major conurbations around Barcelona and Tarragona—a port city and capital of the province of Tarragona, a constituent part of Catalonia—withdrew their support for the typically dominant social democratic, green, neo-communist and neo-populist political formations, which saw *"Ciudadanos"* top the poll. Starkly, while Arrimadas endured all kinds of harassment with great courage and grace, including threats and xenophobic attacks from some secessionist agitators, she failed to meet the expectations that her election had initially raised for many. It is true that she could not cobble together a majority of seats to form a regional government, and she also missed the opportunity to consolidate in opposition to build and develop a solid alternative with winning potential. The strategy imposed by the huge expectations of her party in the parliament in Madrid reduced her role to one of a brave and articulate, but relatively ineffective, resistance, which ended up taking its toll, and her foray into Spanish politics ultimately diluted her role as a plausible alternative to the government of Catalonia. The tremendous crash suffered by *Citizens* party at the regional elections of 14th Feb. 2021, led Arrimadas force almost to irrelevance in Catalonian politics (see Postscript II, p.125). Her role as Spanish leader of the liberal-centrists is not being contested (still), and she seems a long-distance runner by character.

Rufián, meanwhile has always enjoyed a more settled and comfortable political position, rising to prominence with enormous speed to a top position within the ERC hierarchy, the second largest party within the secessionist coalition in the regional government in Catalonia. Rufián easily satisfied all the requirements for ERC leadership, including a traditionalist ideology that is incorporated with a modern and suburban outlook that is central to the movement's image of an inclusive independence for the region. An attractive, somewhat cocky politician, with a sometimes hectoring style, Rufián has a spontaneity, unflappability, and confidence that makes him the envy of many of his peers. Shortly after arriving in Madrid to co-lead the ERC parliamentary group, Rufián became widely known for sometimes brash and theatrical contributions and protestations even during solemn sessions of parliament House and for his outbursts and antics on Twitter which makes him a favourite character for much of the regional and national media. Rufián has rapidly become one of the real characters in Spanish politics, despite sometimes being derided as a shameless populist.

Rufián also endured attacks and harassment and was repudiated as a 'traitor to the homeland' by some opponents—or more specifically as a *"botifler"*[3]—during one of the protests that followed the sentencing of several secessionist leaders by the Supreme Court in downtown Barcelona in October 2019, with the vituperations and accusations he encountered forcing him to leave the demonstration. His political evolution would ultimately lead to Rufián and ERC supporting PSOE in the central government only months later, after agreeing to engage in dialogue with Madrid to find solutions to the entrenched Catalonian situation, which saw him renounce any plan to implement independence, for the time being at least. Rufián knew that this would attract scorn similar to that which he and others had launched against the presidency of the regional government in the stormy days of autumn 2017 on the eve of the declaration of Independence.

Arrimadas and Rufián are therefore well aware of what it means to be subject to threatening intimidation by opponents in the tense cauldron of Catalan politics. Both illustrate, from opposite sides, the degree of confrontation that has been ignited by the divisions created by the secessionist venture. Both Arrimadas and Rufián speak Spanish as their mother tongue and each has an effective and flexible command of the Catalan language of the standard and nature that has become common among the bilingual citizenry with its diverse origins, including those who have experienced compulsory language instruction at school. A version of the language that is usually called "instrumental Catalan" or "*Catanyol: CatSpanish*"[4], this is often seen as a dialect or variant that is on its way to becoming dominant among Catalan language speakers, to the point that it can now often be heard in broadcasts and media debates throughout Spain (102, 111, 124, 125).

Aside from being important politicians of substance, these two figures, from opposing sides of the secessionist debate, are often seen as celebrities within Spanish society. They can be seen fraternising and kissing one another goodbye when leaving television debates. This author would not be surprised if they each acknowledged a bit of mutual admiration for one another as colleagues and perhaps as Catalonian citizens, and both share a common *CatSpanish* character, to a degree at least. This dual national identity feeling, which barely had a relevant political presence until recently and that has often lived on the periphery of the public image in Catalonia, albeit perhaps as a silent majority, has now emerged strongly, partly as a result of the harassment suffered by many during the secessionist push.

THE VOID OF THE CENTRAL SPANISH STATE

A good part of the frailty and impotence that the *CatSpanish* citizenry has felt throughout the secessionist campaign did not originate, it should be noted, in the ceaseless pressure of secessionism, which has indeed been suffocating at many points in the region's recent history. Rather, the origins of the despair within this community lies in Spain's neglect, detachment and ineffectiveness towards the region. There have been many opportunities to acknowledge that a good part of the problem originated in the stubborn and systematic propaganda from a powerful and disobedient regional administration that did not hesitate to use resources to be unfair to Spain while starting along its insurrectional path.

If a central authority receives a claim for sovereignty from a region that can show, moreover, that behind that demand there is a movement of between one and two million people who are willing to sustain the challenge, it seems prudent to take such a bid seriously and to try to counter it on all fronts. This includes all of the tools of engagement, persuasion and intelligence that any government has at its disposal.

What does not help, at all, is to dismiss and disparage any such movement as a social "*souflée*" that never deflated, or as a temporary "*transitory delirium*" that would eventually fade. It's also not helpful either to wait for a spontaneous collapse of the movement due to the fierce internal fights that take place between secessionist factions or to expect that a purely empathetic approach will dissolve the challenge (118). Javier Cercas clearly exemplified the deep *CatSpanish* helplessness on 29 November 2019, upon receiving a distinguished prize for journalism. He personally thanked King Philipp VI for his firm words on 3 October 2017, when the King pointed out that Catalonian citizens that did not want to lose their status as Spanish as well, were not alone, and that the democratic state and the Crown were there to watch over and to protect their rights and to guarantee their freedoms. It was the King himself who had to remember the basics, the most elementary democratic rules that had been neglected by a regional government that blatantly ignored the feelings of the majority of Catalans under their jurisdiction, especially those Catalonian citizens that feel and perceive themselves as Spanish citizens as well.

Such expressions of gratitude to the monarch, coming from a republican and leftist intellectual, should not be surprising, as Cercas had written a mournful protest, not too long before, that expressed the loneliness and helplessness of the *CatSpanish citizenry*.

Javier Cercas, THE GREAT TREASON

El País Semanal, Palos de Ciego, 6 June 2019.[1]

> " . . . The central pact of democratic Catalonia was formulated by his patriarch, Mr. Jordi Pujol[2], in this way: "Anyone who lives and works in Catalonia is Catalan". Hundreds of thousands of immigrants arrived from all over Spain on postwar period, most of them very humble people, believed that pact. My parents believed it, too, and raised their children accordingly. It is true that my mother, 30 years old at that time, who came almost without studies and with five children, does not speak Catalan language, and therefore is one of those people whom the current President of Catalonia called, in a memorable article (69), "scavengers, scorpions, hyenas" and "human-shaped beasts"; but my sisters and I are not like her. We do not only live and work in Catalonia, but we adopted Catalan habits, we immersed

ourselves in Catalonian culture, we learned Catalan language until we became fully bilingual, we married native Catalans, we educated our children in Catalan language and we even contributed to spread Catalan culture.

All in vain. Although we did our best to continue believing that we were Catalonians until recently, in September and October 2017, when everything exploded, we knew without doubt that we were not. Catalans, pure and undeniable Catalonians, were only those citizens who wanted to separate from Spain. Those citizens who don't want it, either because of a sentimental attachment to Spain or because, like myself, we are unable to understand the virtues of a segregation and consider it an unjust and reactionary aspiration, we do not count as Catalans, at least for separatist politicians . . . . For secessionist politicians currently in power, Catalans are not those of us who live and work in Catalonia, but only those who are good Catalans, loyal to the homeland and who vote what needs to be voted. The rest of us are not Catalonians, we do not count, we do not exist. Stop with that illusion: we probably never were Catalans, we never counted, we never existed.

This is what was hidden by the unanimous proclamations of the secessionist movement ("*A single and united people*"; "*The streets will always be our property*" . . .), at the disciplined parades of each 11 September (Catalonian national day), of the so called *revolution of the smiles*. A huge treason, indeed . . . ".

When the Spanish State wanted to react, it was too late. By the time they did, the bulk of influence and public presence, in all areas, was in the hands of the regional administration and secessionist activists. When the King or his Prime Minister scheduled an official visit to Catalonia, it became necessary to mount a security detail that rivalled those deployed by any Western government to support the visit of any American, Chinese or Russian president.

The plight of the *CatSpanish* community also extended to many foreign contexts as Spain's detachment from the increasingly contentious Catalan situation could be easily perceived all around the world. Arguably the most outstanding success for Catalan secessionism lies in the foreign impact of the recent crisis (20). There is almost no way for Spanish or Catalan representatives to attend any international gathering or meeting, at any level, from the loftiest to the most trivial and ordinary, without people bringing up the story of the cosmopolitan and prosperous Catalonia, which aspires to obtain sovereignty through impeccably democratic procedures, in the face of a rigid and authoritarian central government that prevents it and imprisons its leaders. Here, the central administration can be cast as reacting as previous Spanish authorities did in the days of Franco's dictatorship or, even worse, during the Inquisition. The belated and unwieldy "educating" initiatives of Spain's Foreign Affairs Office, the network of "Cervantes Institutes" or the new "Spain Global" Office,[3] have achieved little in this regard. The penetration and dissemination of the Catalonian story of victimisation, meanwhile, has been so effective that it is necessary to recognise and acknowledge the regional government for its effective mobilisation of influence in this regard; the impact and influence over some of the best placed journalists and academics in every corner of the globe is quite remarkable (20).

It is worth asking if an international smear campaign against Spain, launched from the regional authorities in the Basque, Andalusian or Balearic regions, using lavish resources, would have had a similar impact. I suspect that it would have done, and this qualifies a bit the effectiveness of Catalonia's foreign agencies. Arguably, regional rebellions typically receive good press coverage overseas, and even more so if this happen in any territory that is under direct Spain's influence, as the West retains and cherishes memories of ancient insurrections against a vast and arrogant Spanish empire that provided seeds of liberation movements in both Europe and America. However, this does not excuse the apathetic and ineffective response from successive contemporary Spanish governments. On the contrary, it aggravates the diagnosis of a faulty diplomacy because those enduring opinions should be taken for granted with any foreign action or diplomatic intervention.

In any case, it is necessary to recognize that Javier Cercas is an excellent spokesperson for the threats that hang over more than half of Catalonia's population, since the secessionists took command of the regional administration and set themselves on a collision course with Spain. Cercas is a perfect representative because he has already acquired high intellectual status and has global influence. His fictionalised chronicles and novels have lately received international plaudits of the highest order and his work and achievements has been covered by the most distinguished media outlets. Along with the tireless efforts of Mario Vargas-Llosa, the Peruvian Nobel Prize writer, these artists collectively form the best mouthpiece for the anxieties and trepidation afflicting the *CatSpanish* citizenry.

Nevertheless, despite the resonance of their voices and the international relevance that they enjoy, these authors have failed to persuade the bulk of the world's "informed" opinion to support their worldview (20). Their persistent anti-populist and anti-nationalist discourse does not make even a dent in the often blatantly wrong and over-simple vision of the advanced, sophisticated and open Catalonian province that is 'caged' by an authoritarian and oppressive Spanish state that is often presented to the world by supporters of Catalan independence. Typically, the presentation of the Catalans as victims, and the emotive image of "political prisoners" and "exiled" leaders, who are subjected to unremitting persecution by a tyrannical central authority, undermines any sympathy for the *CatSpanish* cause that may arise.

SECESSIONIST TOP LEADERS

This inevitably leads us to Carles Puigdemont, probably the contemporary Spanish politician with the greatest international profile. No other figure in modern Spanish politics has reached the notoriety that he has. On 13 January 2020, Puigdemont secured the latest in a series of victories over the Spanish Courts which have been chasing him since he went into self-imposed exile the weekend following the failed declaration of independence on 27 October 2017, that he himself had proclaimed as president of the regional government of Catalonia. That January day in Strasbourg, Puigdemont participated in a session of the European Parliament, as a representative of the legions of Catalan citizens who had voted for him the previous spring, with all the rights and entitlements as an MEP, despite an outstanding extradition order that had been issued against him by the Spanish Supreme Court.

Puigdemont has spent years avoiding successive lawsuits since his flight into exile, when he crossed the French border incognito and moved on to Belgium, unbeknownst to even most of his former ministers, thereby avoiding arrest and the subsequent trial endured by several members of his deposed government. During his journey as a fugitive, he had to frequently visit police and judicial offices in Brussels, and even went through a brief period of imprisonment in a penitentiary in Northern Germany, where he was held after returning from a trip through the Baltic and Scandinavian countries. However, every time that it looked like international arrest warrants seemed that were going to take effect, he managed to convince foreign judges that his case and cause deserved caution. In Germany, the local Länder Court had agreed, in fact, to hand Puigdemont over to face the accusations of the Spanish Courts for the alleged embezzlement of public funds, but the Spanish judiciary wanted to also try him on charges of rebellion or sedition, as his subordinates in the Catalonian Government had been. In the interim, and while the flurry of petitions and appeals is now delayed within the European Court system, he reaped political success.

Puigdemont has based himself in a dignified presidential residence in Waterloo, on the outskirts of Brussels, which he has managed to convert into the "unofficial", though "de facto" headquarters of the delegation of the Catalonian government to the European institutions. Since this self-imposed "exile" Puigdemont has intervened, with notorious efficiency, in Catalonian and Spanish politics. He frequently leads and directs, via videoconferencing and phone calls, the leading party of the coalition that governed the region since mid-2018. His party finished second only, at the regional election of 14th February 2021. They will probably lose the presidency of the regional Government, but they have secured already the presidency of the regional parliament (See Postscript II (p. 125) for details). He has decisively intervened in the political agreements that allowed the conservative government to be deposed in Madrid and that led, after a year and a half of an interim central government led by the centre-left PSOE party, and ultimately to the consolidation of a social democratic/left populist coalition that now leads the Spanish administration. No one doubts that in the negotiations and exchanges between the Spanish government and the Catalan secessionist government regarding the ongoing dispute in Catalonia, that he will play a vitally important role.[1]

During the hectic autumn of 2017, while I was attending a Psychiatry Congress, in Madrid, I was required to participate in a morning debate on a leading Spanish TV morning show on A3-TV that was led by Susana Griso. A good part of the debate consisted of a series of disparaging comments and withering criticism regarding Puigdemont brought forth by almost all of the other participants. I considered it necessary to remind viewers that Puigdemont was, in fact, a seasoned journalist with a solid track record in local media and in cultural management in Gerona province and that he had become Mayor of his city quite by chance and he was effective and efficient in this role. His arrival to the presidency of the regional government was also came as something of a surprise, having risen to the leadership of the disoriented remains of Convergence (CDC) party and was now preparing to lead the secessionist resistance from Belgium. All told, Puigdemont should be regarded as a person of substance and a highly effective political operator, but nobody took seriously my warnings that he would continue to be a highly relevant actor in Spain's politics. His image as a "persecuted" and "exiled" president is a crucial ingredient of his resonance and of the good press coverage that the secessionist movement consistently receives. His presence and indefatigable activism have done much more to capture the imagination of the European and global media than all the efforts and posturing that the central Spanish authorities could mobilise (20). Puigdemont should be seen as a "global influencer" and never misses the splendid propaganda opportunities that his membership of the European Parliament affords.

The second most important leader of the Catalonian secessionist movement is based primarily in the entertainment industry and his global impact has been and shall remain much more powerful than that of even the most tenacious politician, namely: Mr. Josep Guardiola, the world-renowned and highly decorated current head coach of Manchester City football club. As I wrote in my essay *The Secessionist Passion* (118):

> ... In today's technological and interconnected society both political movements and successful leaderships are forged if they get enough amplification on powerful media supports. To pull up and thrive, the combination of *"prime-time TV plus web-networks spreading"* is compulsory. It is a necessary condition. A must for taking off,

although this does not guarantee getting to the top because competition is brutal. The irresistible emergence of Senator Barack Obama during the Democratic primaries for US presidential nominee, in 2008 elections, established that principle. "Obama" phenomenon, a handsome guy gifted with a sensational and caring voice and armed with the simplest advert of hope ever coined *("Yes, We Can!")* swept the country, became a global icon and generated replicas in many places with minor prophets who tried to emulate him.

That was the reference model for the new messiah: a great and cool guy, elegantly dressed and with a self-assured gaze and posture, using an enveloping and caressing voice to sell naive slogans with a bit of ideological ingenuity. This is enough to conquer the world if TV cameras adore you and social networks spread your psalms.

Recent vintage Catalonian secessionism has enjoyed that leadership for a decade, although exercised, I must say, with discretion. I suspect that the supreme leader of Catalan secessionism has been Mr. Pep Guardiola and I do not greatly exaggerate in saying that he can compete as an equal, in planetary resonance, with Barack Obama. Pep Guardiola took a great Spanish football club, the FC Barcelona, and converted it into the absolute ruler of the world stage in the most popular sport, soccer, over a five-year period (2008-2012). That gave him an unmatched visibility and even today is the world's Most Valuable Coach and one of the most respected football experts, globally. A celebrity of the highest order who also meets the criteria listed at the beginning: "a great and cool guy, elegant demeanour, determined air, using an enveloping and caressing voice to repeat rather naive slogans with a bit of ideological ingenuity". Several international magazines granted him, by the way, the title as the "most elegant and attractive male of the universe", surpassing the splendid stars of Hollywood who often win that award every year.

Since taking the reins of Barça FC team in 2008 and the guarantee of an overwhelming TV presence, Mr. Guardiola began broadcasting signals of full sympathy with aspirations of a sovereign Catalonia that were, at that time, surfacing with force at the region. Departing from a series of sweeping sports successes, he started the habit of expressing himself as a citizen who did not need other identity mark, outside being a Catalonian, to address the entire soccer's world. From the newsrooms of the stadiums of Barça, Manchester, Wembley, Anfield, Emirates, Parc des Princes-Paris, San Siro-Milan, Rome's Olympic, Madrid-Chamartin and many others places, he discussed and argued in Catalan language with the same normality and routine as he did in Italian, English or in Spanish languages. And when it came to talk about his country, his homeland, everyone understood to what place he was referring at. He conveyed to a global audience, but especially to his compatriots, the stubborn message that it was possible to exercise any role or function, without timidity, using a Catalan frame; that this was feasible from any tribune and without sheltering under a Spanish frame. No one had done anything like this—deliberately ignoring Spain, being a Spaniard, with such a persistence and calm elegance —and from places of that impact. His tenacious wit together with his team great victories on the dazzling parades at the most glamorous windows of the planet, helped to convince fellow Catalans with secessionist dreams (majoritarian, probably, among Barça followers and their friendships circles), that everything was possible.

In the massive street demonstration on 11 September 2012 that inaugurated the series of outstanding processions that provided worldwide resonance to "Catalan secessionist challenge," Mr. Guardiola closed the event with a final speech recorded and broadcast from a giant screen. And in the solemn parody of a "self-determination referendum", 11 November 2014, he flew swiftly from Munich to cast his "vote", in downtown Barcelona, offering his image and eager to answer questions to be disseminated *"urbi et orbi"*, expressing his joy and hopes for Catalonian freedom and full sovereignty. A few days earlier, he had led a highly select group of academic and artistic celebrities, publishing a letter of support (51) to the "yearn for democracy" *(sic)* and in favour of Catalan self-determination that was aired by some of the most important newspapers of the globe.

So, the most influential citizen of a community, who had earned a well-deserved place to get listened by the world, was positioning himself giving unequivocal messages in favour of secession. Those are indeed functions of an international ambassador, to say the least.

In the summer of 2015, it was announced that Mr. Guardiola—who was at the time the head coach of German football giants Bayern Munich—had committed himself to the pro-secession political list of the *"Junts pel Sí"* coalition, that had been brought together by both the CDC and ERC parties together with a group of other secessionist movements, for the elections to the autonomous parliament that were scheduled for 27 September of that year. Guardiola was presented as a candidate for a parliamentary seat, occupying the last place on the list. In the following years, and from the even more prominent pulpit of the English Premier League following his move to Manchester, Guardiola has continued to be a high profile spokesperson for Catalan secessionism, taking advantage of his privileged position as a leading figure in world sport.

Guardiola and Puigdemont represent the pinnacle of Catalonia's secessionist leadership, but the movement has created a high-profile and varied group of other celebrities who contribute, from their different positions, to the challenge against the central government in Madrid and to the promotion of the right to self-determination for Catalonia all around the world (20, 31, 118).

MADRID-BARCELONA COMPETITION

Mayor of Barcelona, Ada Colau presides over and dominates the *CatSpanish* world since assuming office in the Catalonian capital in 2015, becoming the first woman to hold the office. Colau does not currently have any prominent competitors or challengers to her prominence and she easily sets the tone of public discourse in the region. A good part of Colau's power flows directly from her occupying the mayoralty of Barcelona, and is not due to any individual outstanding virtues or skills on her part, given the political, economic and social significance that goes with her political leadership of one of the greatest metropolitan conurbations in Europe.

Barcelona city and its dynamic hinterland is the real melting pot of Catalonia and the biggest driver of the varied *CatSpanish* typologies. There is, of course, great diversity with the *CatSpanish* community, but the most frequent forms have taken root within the capital conurbation and in nearby industrial counties. It is there where the population is at its most diverse and where *catanyol*—the variant of the Catalan language that is gaining an increasing presence in literary production and that is often referred to as "*CatSpanish*", by literary critics—is most widely spoken (102, 124, 125).

In the Greater Barcelona area there is also a great sense of pride of belonging to an urban entity of strategic importance. Here, generations of citizens from very varied origins and backgrounds interact, sharing the experience of being inhabitants of a major city. As with any global city, given their style, their habits, and the complicated network of localities through which they move each day, residents of Barcelona often feel themselves as not just citizens of a major conurbation, but also as part of something bigger that can come with a sense of a shared existence and identity. Many cultivate a (mostly playful and health) rivalry with Madrid and believe that Barcelona has little to be envious about when it comes to Spain's capital city. Some even have a tendency to look at it, along with the rest of Spanish cities, with a sense of superiority (that is, when they dare to take a cursory look at them). Inmaculada Colau is a typical example of the stereotypical confidence of Barcelona's citizenry that oozes a progressive and *"a la page"* style and that can be seen as behaving with entitlement and with a high degree of self-assurance, which helps to explain her predicament vis-a-vis the wide network of leftists and left-populist formations that exist across the country (46) and her desire to play an undefined "mid-point" position in the ongoing Catalan secession crisis.

The following pages retrieve a conversation the author had with Cristian Campos* that was reported in *"El Español"* online newspaper in October 2017, *The independent Catalonia would be an extended and catholic Andorra*[1].

The conversation took place the morning after the first proclamation of Catalonian Independence at the autonomous parliament in October 2017, which was followed for two weeks by a series of ultimatums between the Spanish government and the regional authority, amid increasing tensions that culminated with the final proclamation of Independence on 27 October 2017. On that placid morning on the Bellaterra Campus of the UAB (Universitat Autònoma de Barcelona) on the outskirts of the city, in a wide-ranging discussion, we discussed the relevance of the *"Barcelona factor"* to the secessionist push, among many other topics:

You said that the independence movement has interesting characteristics. What do you mean?

I was speaking about an unexpected mass movement that specialists will study for decades. The secessionists mounted a movement that convinced and activated two million citizens. They gave these citizens a well-constructed narrative, with specific objectives and pathways to get them. They organised gigantic demonstrations in the streets. These demonstrations were at the same time civic, festive and aesthetically sensational. Behind them, there were great specialists in advertising, in marketing, in chromatic combinations and mass mobilization.

But that's not the whole story.

They occulted in this way the silencing of the other half of the population. They attempted to establish an absolute domination over the other half of Catalonian citizenry. If you pass over that, they did it well. So well that they captured the main international media, the main TV and broadcasting channels. These media contemplated a peaceful movement and a motivated rebellion characterised by a transversal participation of families from all social classes. The movement had also high chromatic and aesthetic qualities, with flags, t-shirts and performances that changed every year, with different songs, emblems, human castles . . . And that's why it caught media attention, and also the attention of the world intelligentsia.

But have they truly persuaded the intelligentsia?

Nowadays, there are more specialists in mass movements, historians, economists, jurists, sociologists and political scientists, at the best world universities (Oxford, Yale, Cambridge, Harvard, UCLA, Max Planck, Sorbonne . . .), in favour of Catalan secessionist movement, than of the rest of Catalonian citizenry, those who are against secession or in favour of Spain's rights as a democracy.

The secessionists must have been very good, very efficient to get that. They had a great deal of ability to disseminate a doctrine and convince plenty of the best world scholars that they are right.

That Catalonia has the right to exercise self-determination. From influential networks at Research Centers and Universities they have disseminated that story.

If there is so much intellectual excellence in a Catalonia within Spain, what do they complain about?

The narrative is the opposite: "We have achieved this despite Spain. Imagine where we would be without Spain". That's their reasoning line. What they repeat is: "despite the hindrance, the inconveniences, the corrupt and mischievous characteristics of Spanish State, which is slow, distant and prone to indulge on counterproductive legal frameworks, in a competitive environment such as in science, for instance, we have achieved this". Without Spain, they say, we would be the best: "Catalonia would be California or Massachusetts". This is the secessionist storytelling and many scholars across the world believe it.

Utopias always win in comparison with reality.

Then they place a second element in the narrative: Barcelona. There is no need to talk about Universities or advanced Research Centers. Is there any Spanish city, or a city with Spanish influence, able to compete with Barcelona?

Well . . . In what aspect in particular?

In all of them. Who has created and accomplished Barcelona? Catalonian citizens. Barcelona is one of the most attractive cities in the world. No doubt. You get an objective survey and it will always be Barcelona. Not Madrid, Buenos Aires, Seville, Caracas, Lima, Santiago de Chile, Mexico or Bilbao . . . It will be Barcelona. You cannot be a citizen of the world if you do not visit Barcelona often. Because at Barcelona there are many actors at cutting edge of architecture, design, fashion, arts, chemistry, biology, medicine, high-tech. And without the hindrance of Spain, Barcelona would be one of the leading cities of the world. That is the story they tell and everybody believes it. Because it is true.

Is it actually true?

Of course it is. Or at least in a way. Can anyone argue that Barcelona is the most attractive Spanish city? That does not mean that Madrid is not attractive, cosmopolite, diverse, fun, amusing and splendid. But, during the last decades, the presence and relevance of Barcelona in the world has been much higher than Madrid. And that cannot be argued, regardless of indicators used. F.C. Barcelona has also been a much better soccer team than the rest of Spanish and South American teams.

Some people would argue that.

F.C. Barcelona has imposed itself as the dominant team, the most attractive, with most fans, the team who has generated more top players and also some of the football experts most appreciated around the world. Who are secessionists, by the way, in their political preferences. Who did all that? Catalonians. This is the story they tell, and as it is very consistent, it spreads all over the world.

Spain reacted late, and with a wrong diagnosis and a weak and badly built narrative. Spain is perplexed, surprised, doubtful, not understanding the challenge and creating messages that nobody is listening to. Catalonia secession bid made great editorials in the *New York Times, Le Monde, Financial Times, The Guardian, CNN, BBC* . . . "They will not achieve repercussion anywhere", repeated the Spanish media. Please!!: They achieved repercussion everywhere.

With the due respect, maybe you are overrating a simple editorial by a German newspaper in comparison with what Angela Merkel is saying, who is more relevant and influential that all their press means. Or maybe you are mixing up Barcelona touristic attractiveness with its real importance in the international panorama.

It's not only a tourist attraction. I am trying to explain the success that secessionists had all over the world. A different matter is that such success has been gained at the expense of the other half of the population.

Silencing and harassing half of Catalonian citizens. The secessionist plans are imposed and therefore totalitarian, they could sink Barcelona and its creative and innovative capacity. It can sink also the network of smaller Catalan cities. Because Catalonia is not only Barcelona. Now we have had clear signs warning that everything could be wrecked. If you create a movement and in order to win you subjugate half of the population, you place yourself close to disaster and at the edge of a civil conflict. However, the reason why they achieved such an impressive success around the world, is not obvious at all.

The contempt of the opposite side perhaps contributed.

They achieved all that in the open, not within a closed, totalitarian framework. So, the opponents could have reacted. Secessionists did not hid their intentions and goals. From the beginning, they said what their purpose was. The other half of Catalonian population, the subjugated citizens had time to organize themselves. It costs a lot, that's true. The first signal of resistance and forceful power was last Sunday, with the Barcelona "unionist" big street demonstration. This was the first big mobilization in seven years.

All occurred within the framework of the EU. Catalonians were the first in Western European Union to embark on a process of segregation with prospects of success. People from Padania, Bavaria, Sicily, Tirol, Corsica or Brittany, who have as many identity and historical reasons as Catalonians, and who have suffered the same economic crisis, have not succeeded in enacting a comparable movement.

And why the Catalans succeeded and people from Padania did not? Has it to do with genetics?

Because of Spain.

Spain?

This is where Spain enters into the equation. None of these European regions have Autonomous peripheral administrations with as much power and political resources as Spanish regions. Spain democracy is an extremely decentralized and tolerant country. Democratic Spain is probably one of the most open, porous and cosmopolitan countries (remember that I have a tendency to exaggerate a bit: the adjectives, I mean).

I see.

Spain has transferred a high degree of effective power to Regional Governments. The «*Comunidades Autónomas*» are more resourceful and powerful than US federal States, or German Landers in terms of incidence in civic life. The Regional Government decides in which school your children will go, the language in which they will study, how can you transfer your family wealth, which police will impose fines on you . . . Spain has set up a system that, without being nominally federal works as if it was so.

There is no country in Europe that has such a resourceful and varied regional powers with capacity to create and manage local police and judiciary stations, to build large and small hospitals, roads, highways and railways, sports centers, natural parks with special protection . . . . But this is not only valid for Catalonian Government. It is valid for Basque Government, and for Galician, Extremadura, Andalucía Governments . . . The presence of the regional administration in Spain is stunning, it is sensational.

From all the topics discussed at this interview (which was one among many), the most important vector to sustain the successful narrative that the secessionists built and made sold across the whole world, was the enormous influence of Barcelona as a leading European—and global—city.

* * *

THE MADRID-BARCELONA DUALITY

There is not a single other case in Europe of a large peripheral city that competes with and challenges the standing of the capital city in the way that Barcelona does. London, Paris and Berlin have no true domestic adversaries. Neither do Amsterdam, Warsaw, Vienna, Budapest, Stockholm, Lisbon, Copenhagen or Athens. Rome felt Milan breathing down its neck for decades, but ultimately prevailed. The perennial defiance of Barcelona in the face of the powerful magnet of Madrid, acting with its proud conviction as the standard bearer of a different culture, does not occur anywhere else in Europe.

As much as Madrid surprises with its enviable economic and financial vitality, Barcelona has a creativity and dynamism that makes it an inescapable node in terms of its cultural, financial and commercial life, and of course in terms of sport. Barcelona's vitality never lags, even if it sometimes loses some of its potency, even momentarily, due to its domestic tensions (60, 70, 105). Barcelona is powerful and has many comparative advantages to sustain this status. Many of the inhabitants of Barcelona feel in their hearts that they are part of a capital of an alternative world that could give the whole of the Iberian Peninsula a different tone and sense of self from the chaotic and hyperactive Madrid. For these reasons, what happens in Barcelona resonates across Spain as a whole.

The dissonance and disagreements between these two cities have played out periodically over the centuries, although the competition for primacy as a contemporary major hub only became crucial from around the end of nineteenth century. Since then, the two big Spanish 'capitals' have maintained a sustained and seemingly interminable duel that enriches them both, while generating continuous tensions.

Of course, as with other big cities, regardless of the criteria and categorisations that we design, the inhabitants of Barcelona are ultimately heterogeneous. However, arguably the most recognisable product of the great duality in Barcelona, at the time of writing, is the *CatSpanish* identity. Members of this community can speak fluently in Spanish and Catalan. With the knowledge of these two languages comes an association with two rich cultures and traditions, to which you can add the sense of belonging to a leading city in the Western Mediterranean which can bolster the *CatSpanish* identity; and it is well known that whoever dominates a Mediterranean hotspot can contemplate the entire world.

The nature and behaviour of Barcelona's citizens, it should be said, also generates unavoidable tensions with the citizens in inner Catalonia, which is where the bulk of support of secessionism resides. It is clear that the heart of the *CatSpanish* essence and character is based in the Greater Barcelona area. Years ago, this was something that distinguished the city's bourgeois elites from the stiff and stale demeanour of the elites in the rest of Spain, given what was seen as the city's style and discreet elegance, above all. Now, this style has been fused with the irrepressible contribution of the best-settled *"neocharnegos"*—i.e. migrants from the rest of Spain (63) and has ended up permeating the ways of all *CatSpanish*, who now form the majority in the region.

THE VALLS GAMBLE

Manuel Valls—who served as prime minister of France from 2014-2016—had a very good grasp of the Catspanish reality, arriving in Catalan politics in 2019, essentially by himself with only a small group of associates, aiming to capture the mayoralty of Barcelona. His attempt to reorient a brilliant political career, which had brought him from the splendid rooms of the Hôtel Matignon[2] in Paris, to the sober, historical and elegant House of the City in Barcelona, reflects a personal adventure with the tones of an eighteenth-century adventurer. Having failed to reach the Elysée Palace in Paris, after a failed bid for the French presidency in 2017, Valls' transition to the cauldron of municipal politics in the Catalonian capital displays both the individual wit and political acumen of this unique politician.

In the hands of someone with strong leadership skills and clear ambition, the mayor's office in Barcelona can provide an invaluable platform, in terms of global impact and reach, that rivals the most prominent European capitals. By comparison, even the Moncloa Palace[3] in Madrid has been overwhelmed by many internal problems in recent years and has lost momentum to intervene significantly in the major global current issues in the world today.

Ultimately, Valls only managed to consolidate a *"pied a terre"* in the Barcelona City Council, but his vote confirmed Inmaculada Colau as mayor of the city for a new mandate. His tactical flexibility baffled those who had been his allies, but it served to establish him as an important actor on the Spanish scene. The icing on the cake was his famous romance, which unfolded at ultrafast speed, with the upper strata of Barcelona's high bourgeoisie. He will continue to shine among prominent Catalonians, despite his strong associations with France, which for some is cause for suspicion.

Such stigma, that Valls' current or potential rivals can be eager to highlight, may prevent him from rising to greater prominence in Spanish politics. It will be regrettable, because Valls not only captured the often hidden and enormous force of the *CatSpanish* world better than anyone, but he also formulated a clear political action programme to put Barcelona at the centre of the politics of the Iberian Peninsula, and to catapult *CatSpanish* dynamism, bereft of provincial shyness and inhibitions, into its wider European context.

DUAL IDENTITIES
"As Catalan as Spanish"

In surveys regarding political preferences, when inquiring about the *"feelings of belonging"* and questions of national identity, Catalonian citizen are usually compelled to choose between the following alternatives (Table 6.1):

Table 6.1 National identity feelings of Catalonian citizenry

With which of the following statements do you most strongly identify? "I feel…"		
Only Catalan	22,3 per cent	19,2 per cent
More Catalan than Spanish	22,6 per cent	19,5 per cent
As Catalan as Spanish	**39,2 per cent**	**43,6 per cent**
More Spanish than Catalan	4,1 per cent	3,7 per cent
Only Spanish	6,5 per cent	6,7 per cent
Don't Know/NA	5,3 per cent	7,3 per cent

CEO Barom. March 2020 first column CEO Politics Dec. 2019 second column.

The results that appear in Table 6.1 show that the largest segment in Catalonia, is the one that chooses a dual sense of national identity, namely those who: *"feel as Catalan as Spanish"*. Between these two surveys, that were undertaken by the official polling agency of the autonomous government, this cohort represented 43.6 percent and 39.2 percent of those surveyed in December 2019 and March 2020 respectively.

The monochord citizens, those who claimed to feel an identity as *"only Catalan"* oscillated from 19.2 percent to 22.3 percent between these surveys. That group represents the most solid stronghold of the secessionist movement that is long established and seems essentially immovable. In contrast, those who subscribe to a *"Spanish only"* monothematic identity represents only a small minority segment, of between 6.5 percent and 6.7 percent across the surveys. In the CEO Barometer of March 2020, of the 2,000 citizens chosen from across the Catalonian counties who agreed to answer such questions, those who said they felt *"more Catalan than Spanish"* reached 22.6 percent, and *"more Spanish than Catalans"*, 4.1 percent. If we add these two figures to the 39.2 percent that professed a dual/balanced identity, this amounts to 65.9 percent of citizens who possess the ingredients of a shared identity, as either Catalan or Spanish, albeit to varying degrees, but with a predominance of the core dual identity type (i.e. as Catalan as Spanish). At the CEO poll on Political Perceptions, carried out in December 2019 with a similar methodology, with another sample of 1600 citizens, that total figure for those with the ingredients of a dual national identity rose to 66.8 percent.

These measures represent very crude approximations to *"Spanishness"* and *"Catalonianess"* feelings, of course. These studies have received well-deserved criticisms (34, 35, 36, 54, 100, 108), because to more effectively approach and gauge such intimate perceptions with adequate methodological rigour, it would be necessary to use different scales that could disclose various features or components of the phenomenon and to also give a better account of margins of error. However, this way of undertaking surveys, with five neat gradations or closed compartments, has a long tradition, and it has been used in many places at different times (62, 83, 84), and it is the preferred approach for many official survey agencies. This approach can make much more sense when surveys applying similar methods are repeated at regular intervals. In any case, notwithstanding these limitations, there is evidence that this approach reflects, in an acceptable way, the different national affiliations and identities that can be observed in the specific case of Catalonian society (36, 53, 54).

These figures in Table 6.1 have changed little since 2014. The most notable variation sees an increase in the number of citizens moving towards the monochord "*only Catalan*" feeling, at the expense, above all, of the mixed or dual identity (see Figure 8.2, p. 59). Such abrupt oscillation occurred, moreover, over a relatively short interval, between 2012-2014. In the six long years that have elapsed since then, the scenario has hardly changed (90, 91, 92, 100).

This suggests that the strong political push that was launched during the secessionist campaign encountered a hard obstacle that was difficult to overcome. A bloc formed within the population of those that profess to carry ingredients of a "hybrid" Catalan and Spanish identity—that is to say, the core of people with "*CatSpanish*" identity feelings—who, probably, do not see compelling enough reasons for their particular identity to be eroded or annulled. This nucleus of resistance against the pressure of secessionism, in addition, makes up the majority of public sentiment, although it has also displayed a lack of assertiveness and coherence on different occasions at successive elections; arguably, this behaviour is to be expected during a period where the citizenry were asked to go to the ballot box on a number of occasions over a relatively short period of time, with no fewer than five regional elections and five general elections taking place between 2010–2021.

CATSPANISH HYBRIDATION

Being comfortably around 65 percent of the Catalan citizenry indicates that the *CatSpanish* identity goes far beyond the traditional "*charnegos*"[1] and the subsequent "*neocharnegos*" (i.e. the migrants who have arrived more recently form the rest of Spain), which are now beginning to vindicate themselves (7, 63). It is probable that the core *CatSpanish* population, the 35-40 percent that profess a dual and comparable self-identification with both Catalonia and Spain, rests on the complex social fabric that is derived from the huge migratory flow from other Spanish regions, that settled in Catalonia between the 1950s-1970s.

This domestic migration formed the bulk of the industrial working class of most Catalan cities. They laboured in textile factories, in the chemical and automobile complexes and in erecting the enormous urban expansion that underpinned the arrival of the region as a global tourist destination. They filled the suburbs and conurbations around Barcelona and Tarragona, above all, but also the network of medium sized villages throughout Catalonia. They formed the networks of *"the other Catalans"* portrayed by Candel (18), and many got used to bearing the xenophobic nickname of *"charnegos"* with resignation, which emphasised their condition as disinherited outsiders. Today, the derogatory impact of this term has waned to an important extent, and the preferred denigrating nicknames for "outsiders" of Iberian origin are *"ñordos"* or *"españordos"* (7, 63).

In his book *"Yo, charnego"* (2020), López Menacho celebrates the features of continuity between the migratory flows that founded the great demographic and economic expansion of Catalonia in the late 20th century, with the inflows that continue to this day:

> The *neocharnegos* are part of the digital precarious task forces, they are riders of some technological company, valets at Amazon, drivers of Cabify or domestic workers through a mobile *app*. They share a flat. Today we do not arrive in a flood but in a constant trickle, due to the lack of job opportunities at the source. The original *charnegos* lived in suburbs, barracks or neighborhoods with serious deficiencies, crowded into flats, while the *neocharnegos* live in neighborhoods with all services and have their own room. They had no studies and they were factory workers or day laborers, but now the *neocharnegos* have completed secondary, if not higher, studies and work at the service sector mainly. They no longer arrive by train but on low-cost flights. Catalonia is no longer its first destination, it comes behind countries like Germany, England or Ireland.

Catalonia today, and especially Barcelona, ends up being a destination that fulfills the expectations of the domestic migrant, a sort of modern Hollywood for the Andalusian, Murcian or Extremaduran youth, main generators of *charneguism*. It is the place where dreams come true, basically, because it has more opportunities in all professional sectors . . . Today, in Catalonia there are around 1,200,000 foreigners from all over the world. Only the internal migration of the first *charnegos* would equal what now represents the foreign migration

The architecture of the city, its buildings, its urban furniture, has nothing to do with what it was. There are suburbs (and within these, neighborhoods) especially prone to receive foreign people. And they do it for historical reasons. In some way, the new *charnegos* generations take advantage of the history of their predecessors, walking their same path . . . ; This is, by far, the greatest heritage from old *charnegos*: a historical legacy in the form of brick and asphalt, together with survival manuals . . . ; There was a normalization of success in those *charnego* neighborhoods; but just as important as that, was to make the silent work that created the society that we found today: workers and modest merchants, school teachers . . . . a reason for celebration. Women and men converting a wasteland into an ambulatory with the strength of the neighborhood links, who faced the bulldozers, who cut the streets . . . .; Barcelona citizenry who, after exhausting themselves in the assembly lines, in the roar of factories, drew strength from their own poverty to turn life into democracy

The *neocharnego* no longer has to do such extra effort, because the work is already done. His perspective is another, more oriented to the strengthening of the socioeconomic conquest that the predecessors began, often without even knowing it. And the nickname *charnego* no longer points in the way it did. Now, fear of foreigners and xenophobia targets other migrant groups. The Arab community receives prejudice whenever there is an attack in the first world . . . ; the new migrations come to occupy the space that *charneguism* had in the seventies and eighties. In Olot and Vic, two of the most representative villages in inland Catalonia, the migrant population is 22 percent and 33 percent respectively. Guissona, Castelló d'Empúries, Salt or Sant Pere Pescador have a percentage close to or greater than 40 percent of migrants. Of all the nationalities, Moroccan and Romanian are the majority . . . ; old *charnegos* have worked many times as a glue: they understand both migrant and natives. They understand those who want to conquer their destiny, but also show a tendency to protect a space that they have made their own . . .

The hybridization processes within those with *CatSpanish* identities, however, go much further and encompass a much greater proportion of the citizenry than those bounded by *charneguism* and *neocharneguism* together.

We have seen that there are approximately 25 percent of individuals who report a dual identity with biased weights, with slightly more than 20 percent with a preference for the Catalan side (*"more Catalan than Spanish"*), and 5 percent with a firm bias towards Spanishness (*"more Spanish than Catalan"*) (see Table 6.1). This is an obviously *CatSpanish* cohort that would require a lot of work and care to be described in any detail. Moreover, it would come as no surprise if some of those who impulsively jumped on the bandwagon of the *"Catalan only"* monochord identity during the climax of the secessionist push, might in fact be found to harbour remnants of *CatSpanish* identity as well.

But all of these are merely targets for ulterior and systematic investigations that take time to undertake. Thorough inquiries must explore not only descriptions based on national identity feelings during opinion surveys, but also objective measures relating to economic stratification, educational segmentation, and the levels or territorial distribution of the citizenry through urban, suburban and rural areas. The studies already carried out on the different degrees of economic mobility in Catalonia, based on aggregations of native or imported surnames (27, 52), or those detecting genetic traces of ancient or modern migratory flows (15, 104), and their differential distribution according to different surnames (114), predict a splendid and potentially challenging variability.

FOREIGNERS

Alongside the citizenry who can trace their roots in the Catalan region over decades, there are truly outsiders who have arrived to Catalonia especially over more recent decades. Some were attracted by the economic boom that took place around the turn of the millennium and in the wake of the 1992 Olympics, when Barcelona became a worldwide tourist attraction, and others by the consolidation of Catalonia as a major economic hub in the Western Mediterranean, despite the aftermath of the financial crash of 2008-2012.

In total, foreigners now exceed more than one million residents according to the latest official records[2], within the region's total population of 7.5 million. Those coming from elsewhere in the European Union, as well as from North African regions and South America, dominate this cohort with proportions of above 25 percent for each of these three groups, followed not far behind by migrants from Asia, who already make up close to 15 percent of the foreign population.

There is, therefore, a huge contingent of foreign but internal "observers" to what has been recently going on in Catalonia. The identification of newcomers to the region with *CatSpanish* sentiments is naturally easier for Latin-Americans, for obvious reasons, given the range of linguistic, historical and cultural affinities that these cohorts share, and identifying as *CatSpanish* will be less natural for the rest. All this is widely known, and the official agencies of the secessionist government devote substantial resources to trying to cultivate links with these communities, hoping to form bonds with those citizens who decide to establish themselves and their families within the region. To better understand these variations will require detailed studies, involving each of these different communities, to discern their potential weight and influence over the secessionist and unionist forces.

CANTONALISM AND CAINISM IN SPAIN

A point that rarely ceases to amaze me is how the force of Spanish influence is maintained across the successive generations of *CatSpanish* citizens, because reasons to repudiate the national identity that Spain offers are far from lacking. Here I'm not talking about the reasons most often referred to, including: corruption, patronage and the inefficiency of many gears of the state machinery and its surrogates in the regional administrations; the picaresque and shameless advantage afforded to a small portion of Spaniards; the masquerade of sham progressivism that so often appear in every corner of the Iberian Peninsula. No, it's not all of this that truly demoralises, because any dispassionate observer knows that these are widespread vices and that there is no guarantee that the Catalonian citizenry could offer an improved profile (117, 118), as has been shown in the past.

What is truly hopeless though, is the powerful Iberian tendency towards stark and savage sectarianism, and towards fratricidal and seemingly hopeless factionalism. The past years have shed much light on such propensities. The most abrupt encounters have occurred, precisely, around the discrepancies over the "Catalan secessionist bid" and have been stirred by the spokespersons from across all political formations and have often been carried out with ferocity and bitterness.

This belligerence at the top contrasts with the remarkable patience that most Spanish citizens have shown in the face of mistreatment and insults that came in abundance from Catalonia. The Spanish people have known how to metabolize with commendable stamina the unpleasant drip-drip of expressions of contempt coming from many parts of Catalan society. Except for the sporadic outbursts and cries of *"A por ellos!" ("Go for them!")*, that appeared in some small corners of Spanish society during the stormy days of Autumn 2017, as police patrols were dispatched towards Catalonia, what predominated overall was a sense of containment and prudence. This stoicism is notable, as it must be remembered, that on many occasions the most disdainful and demeaning comments came from the highest echelons of Catalan society. There is a detailed record of examples of hate speech from prominent Catalonian politicians, including the President of the Regional Government and of the Autonomous Parliament (69), towards their Spanish neighbours.

The phlegmatic reaction of ordinary Spaniards who, while airing their understandable fatigue at the reiteration of the "monotopic", preferred to receive any insult with patience. However, the widespread sense within Spanish society that *"these Catalans are very peculiar and stubborn, you know, but the tantrum over the secession will end up"* was not taken up by the Spanish leadership. On the contrary, there has been much sectarian rhetoric emanating from leading figures in Spain that is designed to manipulate the situation and its inherent tension so as to accentuate differences and to earn political advantage.

Most Catalonian citizens lived with great relief and undisguised hope during the short period between 28 October 2017 and 2 June 2018. In other words: the period that Article 155 of the Spanish Constitution[1] ruled in Catalonia, with the suspension of the autonomous government and with all power being transferred to the central administration. This was a period of relief for many after long years of tension. While public spaces were filled with yellow ribbons (the preferred symbol of the secessionists) and protest insignia calling for the immediate release of the imprisoned leaders, daily life became much more bearable for many citizens, as the succession of countless clashes between the autonomous and central governments ceased to dominate public discourse. Everything seemed to flow with unusual normality during this time and it was soon realised that the concerted action of the big national parties could curb a regional drift that had become a threat to civil harmony in the region.

But that confluence between major Spanish parties to redirect what many proclaimed to be the country's biggest problem—an attempt of secession by a constituent part of the nation—was broken, as soon as a new horizon appeared, that allowed other alliances to be established to seize power in Madrid. The left-wing central governments that have since been installed, one with PSOE leading a minority government, which was followed by a social democratic/left populist coalition, established points of contact with the secessionist movement given that they rely on the support of the regional parties to stay in power. Since then, Spanish factionalism has been accentuated to surprising, and inexact, extremes: on the one hand, there are the *"open-minded"* Spaniards—tolerant, egalitarian and cosmopolitan (often the self-identified 'left' faction)—and on the other hand, there are the *"authoritarian and reactionary"* Spaniards (the right, by any traditional definition), even though these are inappropriate and insufficient stereotypes. Support for the centre or liberal opinion has almost totally evaporated. Meanwhile, while the Catalan and Basque secessionists have used these polarising shifts to remarkably good effect, by shoring up support among their members, a further outcome of this climate has been the appearance of a new political formation on the far-right, which has established itself vigorously in recent elections (94).

The most immediate and direct losers of this merciless confrontation between the two antagonistic and irreconcilable Spanish poles, are the *CatSpanish* citizens themselves. The large segment of the Catalonian population with feelings of dual identity, feeling both Catalan and Spanish, and who cultivate aspirations of continuing with these hybrid ways of living and functioning, observe how the "Catalan problem" once again sees them caught in the crossfire between the two different factions.

Mr. Andreu Mas Colell, an oracle for secessionism and who arouses a curious veneration among many academic audiences within Spain, clearly illustrated this at the end of 2019, in "El País"[2]. To bless the formation of the left-wing social democratic/left populist coalition supported by Catalan secessionist forces, he stated the following (72):

> ... The Catalan political conflict is entering a phase of negotiation, formal and informal. Now it matters that, collectively, we are not mistaken again....; In the negotiation we have four sensitivities, which I'm not trying to associate with political parties. On the one hand, we have, in Catalonia, the secessionists aiming for full sovereignty, for whom a nation must have a State, and also those citizens who also claim for sovereignty but who can relativize secession and put more emphasis on the preservation of the nation and self-government (the "*sobiranistes aindependentistes*"). On the other hand, in Spain scenario we would have dialogue and non-dialogue sensitivities. The last two general elections seem to demonstrate that the dialogue field is majoritarian, albeit narrowly.
>
> I think that the strategic interaction of these four sensitivities should give way to a government that fosters dialogue and negotiation. From the Catalan side, promoting it is what is technically called a dominant strategy: it is the best in any circumstance. For "*sobiranistes aindependentistes*" their natural attitude will be to favour the formation of this Government. The secessionists must do the same because, if they are so convinced of the failure of negotiation, it will be by demonstrating that they are willing to negotiate—and, I add, limiting themselves to ordered and non-disruptive protests—they will gain reasons and expand the basis for the next phase of the dispute. Obviously, the dialogue strategy will then also be the best for Spanish dialogue sensitivity ...

Note that in this apparently innocuous approach, the actors are reduced to two pre-defined poles on opposing both sides, that together fill the strategic board: in Catalonia there are only citizens demanding sovereignty, while the rest simply do not exist, while in Spain there is only one type of practicable people, namely those who are open to dialogue. For Mas Colell, the rest may perhaps exist, but they do not count.

Reducing the complexity of actors in any social conflict to a simple caricature of opposing strategies of cooperation or non-cooperation is a less and less acceptable approach that is taken by some economists and scholars. In general, such commentators are surprised if someone with executive responsibilities decides to listen to them. A conspicuous example of this was how the former minister of regional government Ms. Clara Ponsatí would use strategies based on "game theory" by the secessionist government to explain the Catalan situation. The bemused and often frosty reception she experienced for such analyses in the media and public discourse led her to return rather quickly to her university teaching in Scotland.

The abovementioned approach of Mr. Mas Colell is outstanding, to say the least, in how it implies erasing, at a stroke, the biggest segment of Catalonian citizens: those devoid of sovereignty aspirations and who never stated that their hopes or preferences included to "*preserve the nation*". But if, in addition to that, it is openly proposed that in Spain there are only two classes of subjects, namely those open to dialogue and those more primitive ones who probably have not reached the evolutionary stage that permits the exchange of opinions and arguments, the analysis acquires worrying and scandalous overtones.

This is more than worrisome, in fact. In a subsequent morning debate on Madrid SER radio[3], it turned out that there was unanimity among the participants that Mr. Mas Colell's homily was a sensational and important contribution to the public debate. Upon hearing this, the temptation to escape urgently from Spain was almost instantly aroused.

LONGITUDINAL PROFILES OF CATALONIAN CITIZENRY[1]

At the middle of this journey through the features and nuances of the *CatSpanish* world, it is convenient to reflect again on the core of the initial conflict, namely the fracture of Catalonian citizenry into two opposing sides that has been created by the secessionist campaign. It must be remembered from the outset that, when a political conflict focuses on a nodal and non-negotiable discrepancy between the pro-secession and anti-secession factions, as is the case here, the chances of digging a trench between two strongly opposing sides is extremely high. And when that happens in a context where it is easy to draw lines of friction or cleavage that run alongside elements of clear ethnocultural or social signifiers (i.e. language, ancestry, socio-economic status), then the possibilities that such opposing sides can get stuck in positions that are ready for open combat is even higher (1, 40, 41, 58, 81).

The recent boom of chronicles, essays, TV productions and plays that have been precipitated by the secessionist bid may serve as a measure of the extent of confrontation that exists within Catalan society as well as in wider Spanish society. No similar flood of self-interrogation has occurred in Spain over the last eighty years. It is clear that this entrenchment will continue to reverberate for years. This situation has long surpassed the cultural productions associated with the deadly Basque conflict, starring ETA, during the last quarter of the twentieth century, and perhaps it might come close to the cultural aftereffects left by the immense shock of the Spanish Civil War of 1936-1939, or the crisis of the 1898 Spanish-American War, which saw the country lose the final remnants of Empire, including Cuba and the Philippines.

The main aim behind the several studies that preceded this essay (89, 90, 91, 92) was to accrue a series of longitudinal findings that could shed light on important vectors that primed the appearance of the antagonistic fissure between unionist and secessionist communities in the Catalan region. By building upon the complete series of data from official CEO polls, the evolving changes of national identity feelings ("*sense of belonging*"), throughout the period 2006-2020, are displayed in relation to other variables. The longitudinal analyses included 92,038 respondents from 47 surveys and several procedural tools were also applied to detect important *breaking points* linked to singular events that might have accentuated the ongoing and intense polarization around the issue of secession.

Firstly, attention is focused on any variations of *sense of belonging* feelings (national identity) across two significant segments of Catalan citizens, namely: those whose family language is Catalan and. those whose family language is Spanish. This is a crucial starting point, as previous findings, either from survey data or from electoral results, had long-established the priority of this ethnolinguistic cleavage origins (8, 33, 55, 75, 78, 79, 88). Secondly, attention is focused on the assessment of the evolving changes of *sense of belonging* depending on media preferences—that is, between the official TV and radio outlets controlled the regional government (broadcasting exclusively in Catalan language), and any other TV and radio outlets, the importance of which had also been established previously (43, 88, 119). Since media consumption trends and language/ascendancy origins are closely interrelated within the region, the present discussion highlights the role played by the interactions between these ingredients on the deepening of the fissure that separates secessionists and unionists. The role of other relevant economic and social transitions that contribute to the pattern of traits that currently characterise the political entrenchment between secessionists and unionists is also explored.

The idea behind this detailed itinerary through an unexpected, serious and stagnated political crises, at the heart of a European democracy, was to try to illuminate relevant pathways that may help not only to understand the origins and development of the conflict, but also to hopefully to reduce or stymie some of its more worrying legacies.

Figure 8.1 displays the evolving profiles of national identity feelings ("*sense of belonging*") along the period, 2006-2020. This is a qualitative variable with six distinct values at these surveys: "*only Spanish*", "*more Spanish than Catalan*", "*as Spanish as Catalan*", "*more Catalan than Spanish*", "*only Catalan*" and "DK/NA" (don't know or no answers). Percentages were estimated from responses to 47 surveys over the period 2006–2020 on sample sizes of between 1500 and 2500 persons (one survey in 2017, exceptionally had only 1338 participants), with a total of 92,038 respondents.

Throughout these years, the total increase in those who feel "*only Catalans*" reached 13 percent, while the drop in the number of citizens who feel "*as Spanish as Catalan*" reached 7 percent, signalling a substantial variation towards narrowing the relevance of dual *CatSpanish* national identity feelings.

The more remarkable facts in Figure 8.1 are the changes around 2012 regarding the size of the two critical segments defined by national identity. In that year, the dual national identity group "*as Spanish as Catalan*" initiated an abrupt descent of more than 15 percentage points from which it has not yet recovered, while the single national identity "*only Catalan*" group saw an abrupt escalation of more than 15 points which has not yet been reversed. Such variations among segments that are so critical for cohesion of the whole society clearly demanded further inspection involving other variables.

The marks at Figure 8.1 signal events that might have been relevant to any understanding of the evolution of the variables throughout the

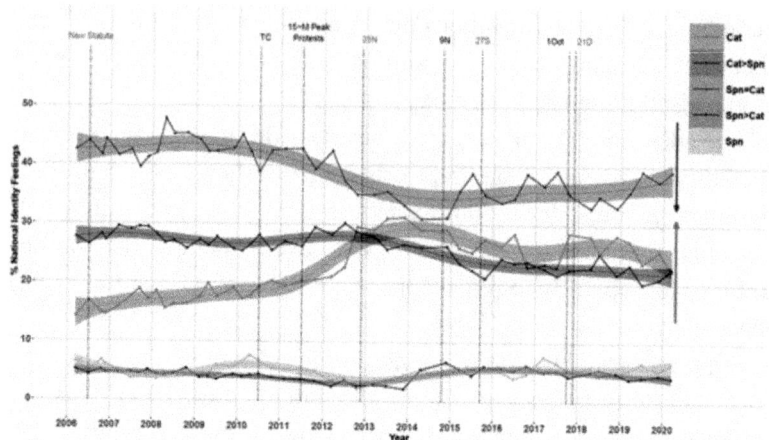

Figure 8.1 National identity feelings (sense of belonging) for all Catalonian population (2006-2020). Elaborated from CEO-Barometer survey microdata. Observe a clear reduction of percentages of people with dual identity "equal Spanish than Catalan" (top segment line), and the increase of percentage of people with a single identity "only Catalan" (third segment line, at the start). The proportion of people with single identity "only Spanish" (bottom segment line) remained stable. The proportion of "DK/NA" is omitted.

period. This included: the date when a new home rule statute was approved (New Statute 2006); the resolution of the Spanish High Court (Tribunal Constitutional-TC) that sanctioned 14 articles (from a total of 223) as contrary to the Spanish Constitution and restricted the preamble and another 27 articles (June 2010); the high point of the protests of the 15M social movement (15M Peak Protests, June 2011); the regional elections of 25 November 2012 (25N); the illegal consultation regarding independence of 9 November 2014 (9N); the regional elections of 27 September 2015, (27S); the illegal referendum regarding secession on 1 October 2017 (1 Oct) and the regional elections of 21 December 2017 (21D). The crucial breaking points detected by the package, available for R, ecp[2], are marked as solid-wide vertical lines within following the plots.

These evolving changes become more evident when studying national identity feelings in the segments obtained by dividing citizens through their family/mother language[3]. There are two quantitatively important linguistic groups, within the region (Figures 8.2 and 8.3), namely: citizens whose family language is Catalan and citizens whose family language is Spanish, representing 35.4 percent and 57.1 percent of total population respectively (at the last included survey, March 2020). People with both Spanish and Catalan as family/mother languages represented an average of 4.3 percent of the population, while other cases were negligible. The small group whose family/mother language was "both" (Spanish and Catalan), exhibited an intermediate behaviour, so its graph has been omitted.

For the family-language Catalan group, the crucial breaking points on national identity feelings appeared between the second and third CEO 2010 surveys (decimal number approximately 2010.4 on the graph), and the second and third CEO 2012 surveys (decimal number 2012.65). For the family-language Spanish group Figure 8.3, the breaking points in these profiles were between the second and third CEO 2011 surveys (decimal number 2011.65), and the second and

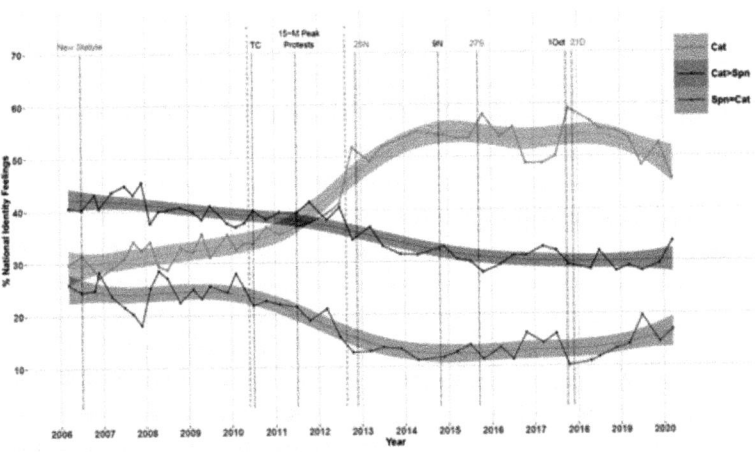

Figure 8.2 National identity feelings (sense of belonging) among citizens with family/mother language Catalan (35.4 per cent of total population, March 2020 survey). *Source*: Derived from CEO-Barometer survey microdata. Observe the spectacular rise of the single identity "only Catalan" (in middle segment line, at the start), which began around 2010. Observe the opposite trend for the dual identity "as Spanish as Catalan" (in bottom segment line) over the same period.

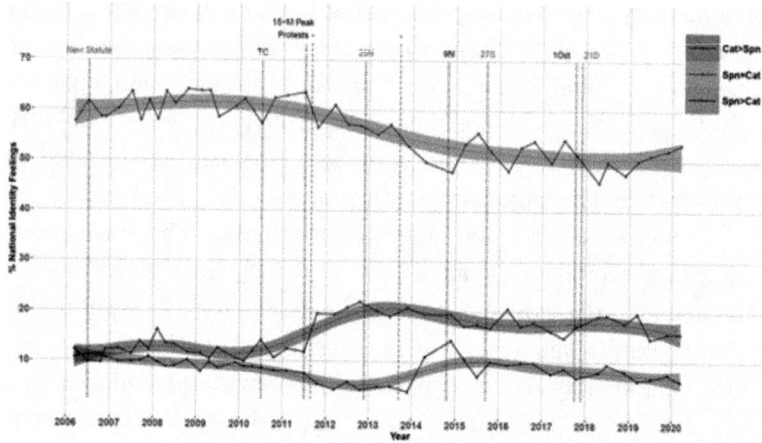

Figure 8.3 National identity feelings (sense of belonging) among citizens with family/mother language Spanish (57.1 per cent of total population, March 2020 survey). *Source*: Elaborated from CEO-Barometer survey microdata. Observe a moderate decrement of dual identity "as Spanish as Catalan" (top segment line)

the third CEO 2013 surveys (decimal number 2013.7). The more outstanding change appeared within the family-language Catalan group Figure 8.2, which jumped towards a monolithic *"Catalan only"* identity, notably around the regional elections of 25 November 2012.

IMPORTANT MEDIA EFFECTS ON THE CURRENT SOCIAL DIVISION

The relevance of media preferences was also analysed. The *news variable* was built taking into account the answers relating to whether respondents preferred to obtain news through regional public media (TV or radio broadcasting exclusively in the Catalan language) or via other media. This is a dichotomous variable with two possible values: "regional" or "other". The first analysis (Figure 8.4) were directed towards the variations in national identity as "only Catalan", distinguishing also between sub-groups that had Catalan as the family-language and Spanish as the family-language

There were important changes relating to *"only Catalan"* national identity throughout the period, which were dependent on family/mother language but also on having been exposed to regional public media or not. The relevance of these covariations where highlighted through robust statistical contrasts.

The same analysis was repeated for variations on respondents whose national identity was *"as Spanish as Catalan"* (Figure 8.5), obtaining also substantial distinctions dependent on family language and media preferences.

By repeating the analysis relating to general public media or private plus public media, excluding the regional outlets, no increased association appeared with respect to feelings of *"only Spanish"* national identity, as is illustrated in Figure 8.6. This shows the notorious stability of feelings of national identity within the segment of Catalonians (more than 30 percent, according to these surveys),

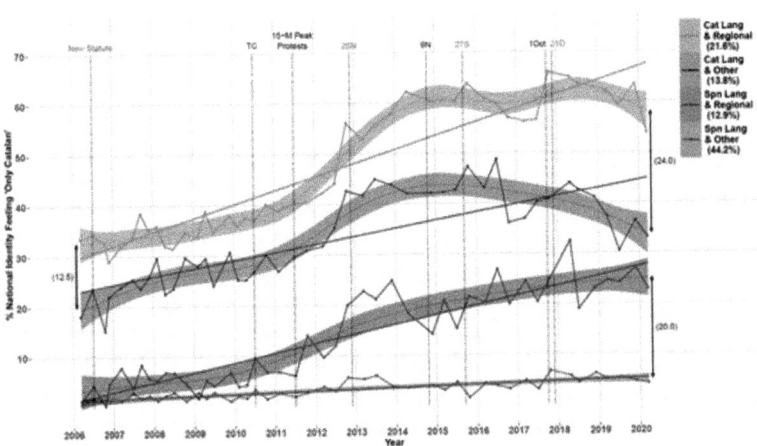

Figure 8.4 Changes in "only Catalan" national identities in different population segments depending on family/mother language and media preferences (i.e. public regional media or not). *Source*: Elaborated from CEO-Barometer survey microdata. In 2006, "only Catalan" national identity amounted to 14.2 per cent of the entire population, whereas at the last survey (March 2020), this had reached 22.2 per cent. Attached to each label, on the right column, appear the percentages of each group in the March 2020 survey. Two top segment lines: family language Catalan; bottom segment lines: family language Spanish.

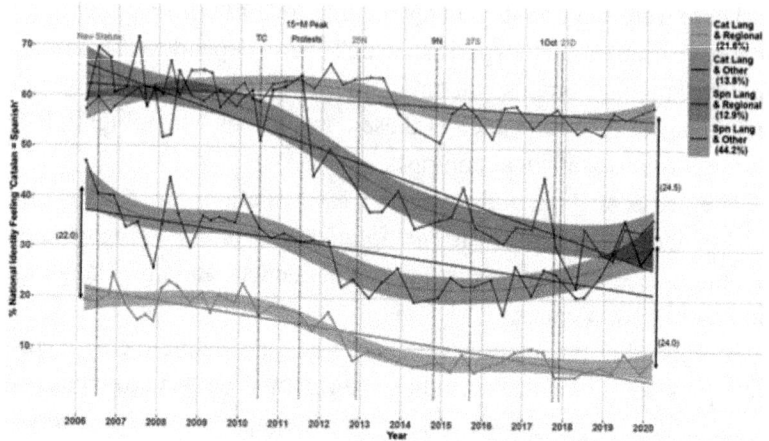

Figure 8.5 Changes in "as Spanish as Catalan" national identity in different population segments obtained by considering family/mother language and news preferences (i.e. consumption of public regional media or not). *Source*: Elaborated from CEO-Barometer survey microdata. In 2006, "as Spanish as Catalan" identity was 42.5 per cent of the entire population, whereas in the last survey (March 2020), this had dropped to 39.1 per cent. Attached to each label, on the right column, appear the percentages of each group in the March 2020 survey. Two top segment lines: family language Spanish; bottom segment lines: family language Catalan.

relating to people who claimed to follow political news through Spanish TV channels and radio broadcasting. Hence, although no media is ever truly scrupulously neutral, the strong biasing influence of regional media on national identification is absent in this case.

By combining all these measures, a summary of the notorious gap between secessionists and unionists was built that was dependent on questions of both family language and the communication bubbles that are created by following/not following regional media (Figure 8.7). This was followed by an estimation of the probability of being either secessionist or non-secessionist using only these ingredients. The Figure 8.7 shows that depending on the family/mother language (Catalan vs Spanish) and taking into account whether a citizen follows the news through public regional media or not, it is possible to predict the probability of supporting secession in a hypothetical referendum with a magnitude of 16.5 percent for

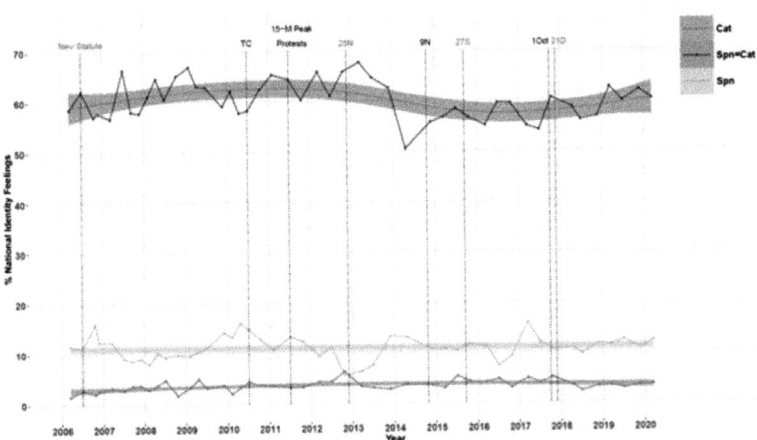

Figure 8.6 Evolution of feelings of national identity (sense of belonging) for Catalonians who follow news from Spanish broadcasters (e.g. TVE, A3, TV5, La Cuatro, La Sexta). *Source*: Elaborated from CEO-Barometer survey microdata. This segment was 35.4 per cent of the entire population in 2006, and in the last survey (March 2020) it was 32.6 per cent. Notably that there is no evidence of polarization dependent on media following here. Top segment line: *As Spanish as Catalan* identity.

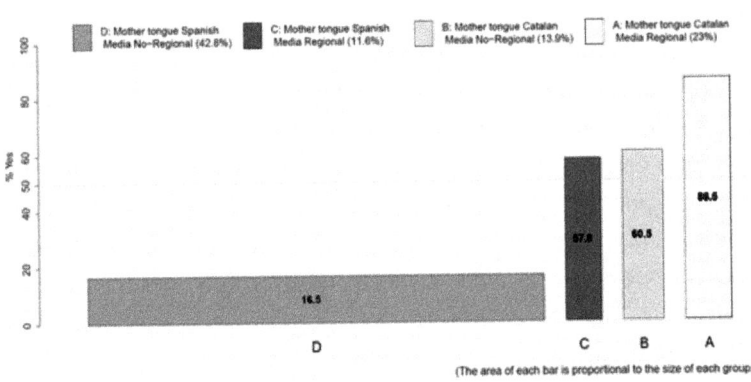

Figure 8.7 Barplot of the proportion of support for secession for the combinations of language and exposure (or not) to public regional media. *Source*: Elaborated from CEO-Barometer survey microdata. The area of each bar is proportional to the population size of each group, while the numbers inside each bar reflect the percentage support for secession. Population percentages appearing besides labels at the top of the Figure are the average values within the period 2015-2020.

"D" segment (Catalonians with family language as Spanish who do not follow regional media), to a magnitude of 86.5 percent for the "A" segment (Catalonians with family language Catalan who follow news through regional media).

Taking this together, each of these evolving profiles has helped to define, with consistency, the nature of unionist and secessionist citizenship in Catalonia over the past decade.

Solid secessionists make up approximately 23 percent of the population, and the bulk is made up of a population with family language Catalan who prefer to follow the news and political debate through the regional public media (TV3 and CatRadio). Solid unionists reach 43 percent and are citizens with Spanish as family-mother tongue who follow the news and political debates in the Spain-wide media outlets. There is a considerable cohort of 14 percent that is made up of Catalans of origin and language, who prefer the Spain-wide media and 12 percent of Spanish-speaking citizens, who prefer the regional media. Taken together, this 26 percent could opt for one side or the other when it comes to secession, depending on a range of factors and the political context, and the current support for secession in this cohort stands at around 50 percent.

That is to say, it can be estimated that there are some 64-68 percent of *CatSpanish* citizenry in Catalonia in total. A third of them have serious doubts, however, regarding the merits of secession.

In front of them, there are 23-27 percent of irreducible Catalonians who are allergic to any attempt at rapprochement with Spain. Consequently, the sustained tension between supporters and opponents of secession is always there more or less entrenched (see Figure 8.7). This leaves between 5-10 percent who are 'floating voters' or are totally uninterested in the debate.

PRIVILEGED REBELS: ECONOMIC AND WELL-BEING DIFFERENCES BEHIND THE SECESSIONIST PUSH

The relevance of basic socioeconomic factors on preferences for secession had been highlighted by Llaneras (66) using data from CEO surveys during the crucial months of Autumn 2017 around the time of the latest illegal self-determination referendum. Secession appealed mostly to native Catalans, and was highest among citizens born in Catalonia and with at least one Catalan-born parent, with a maximum (75 percent) for those with long native ascendancy. Among citizens coming from abroad or from other Spanish regions, and those born within the region from migrant parents, secession was not attractive at all (CEO Barometer July 2017). The divide depended also on income, as citizens with higher incomes and those who responded "we live comfortably" were the ones most positively disposed towards secession. Meanwhile, most people with the lowest salaries and those disclosing "many economic difficulties" were predominately against secession. Maza et al (75)'s multivariate analysis of voting behaviour at regional elections of 21 December 2017, fully confirmed the priority of ascendancy origins to explain the results, while diminishing the relevance of economic factors (see also results: 11, 33, 107). Moreover, using CEO surveys at 2011-2013 period, Boylan (13) had already shown that national identity feelings (i.e. being a native or an assimilated Catalonian) was a much stronger predictor of the desire for secession, than grievances resulting from perceived unfair fiscal treatment or other economic and political factors.

Reflecting household net income levels among citizens with family/mother language Catalan and those with family/mother language Spanish, Figure 8.8 displays estimations of the median household net incomes for each linguistic segment throughout the period 2006–2020. Citizens with family language Catalan exhibited higher household incomes throughout the period compared with citizens with family language Spanish. The trend line suggests that the economic crisis increased the magnitude of this inequality.

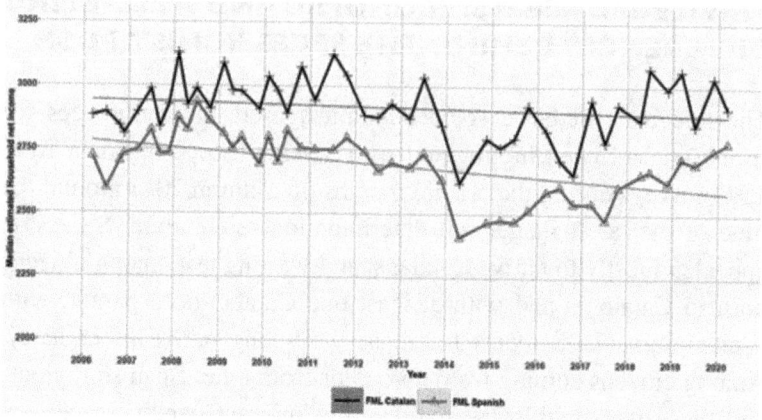

Figure 8.8 Figure 14. Evolution of median estimates of household net income among citizens with family/mother language Catalan compared to those with family/mother language Spanish. Observe the differences between these groups and how they increase throughout the economic crisis. Primary source: CEO Barometers 2006–2020. FML: Family/mother language (FML Spanish: 56 per cent of the Catalonian citizenry; FML Catalan: 36 per cent; FML both Catalan and Spanish 6 per cent; Source: EULP2018-Enquesta Usos lingüístics de la població, Institut Estadístic Catalunya; (www.idescat.cat/pub/?id=eulp)

The evolution of incomes shows that the most intense effects of the economic crisis, during the period 2010 to 2018, were delayed as was the case in the rest of Spain, while family language Catalan households had already fully recovered by 2017.

Figure 8.9 displays the combination of the binary variable "household net income </>3000€/month" with the two "family/mother language" segments showing their covariation with support for secession in a hypothetical referendum. Results depict a very strong effect, again, of family language, with Catalan-speaking homes being predominantly secessionist while Spanish-speaking households were more predominately unionist. Income levels also had a minor effect on the probability of support for secession, as wealthier households reported higher support for secession in both the family language segments. The difference was even clearer within the Spanish-speaking group, even though it started from an extremely low level of support

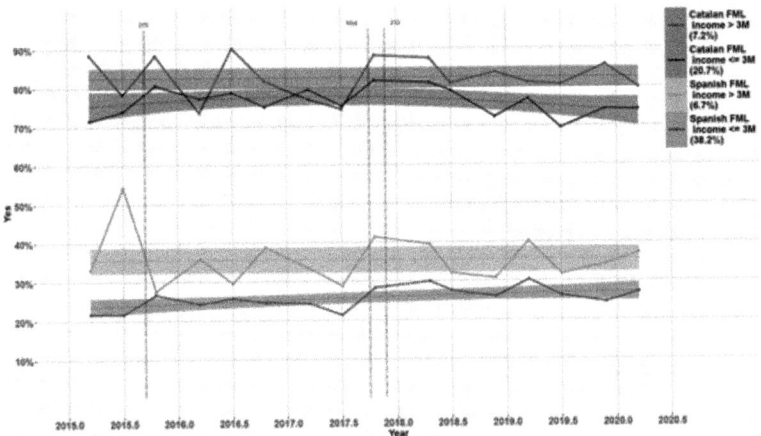

Figure 8.9 Covariation of household net incomes and family/mother language on support of secession. *Source*: Elaborated from CEO Barometers survey microdata. In addition to the effects of family/mother language, observe the distinctive effect of incomes levels within groups, especially within Spanish-speaking households. Also, attached to each label, there is the population percentage for each group from the March 2020 survey. FML: Family-Mother Language. 1M = one thousand Euros/month.

for secession. That is, the economically well-situated also predominate among those few Spanish-speaking secessionist households.

The covariations of "Household net income </>3000€/month" and "family/mother language" with "national identity feelings" for the "*only Catalan*" and "*as Catalan as Spanish*" segments appear in Figures 8.10 and 8.11. The effects of income levels were much more modest than those obtained for following/not following regional media (see Figures 8.4 and 8.5). Very modest effects were also obtained, on the same contrasts, for the tiny segment of "*Only Spanish*" (Figure 8.12, p. 69).

Finally, Figure 8.13, (p. 70) shows comparisons of support for secession among different groups obtained considering their reported economic resistance limits (in months), in case of economic breakdown. Results showed that support for secessionism increased with higher resistance limits, as people with higher financial

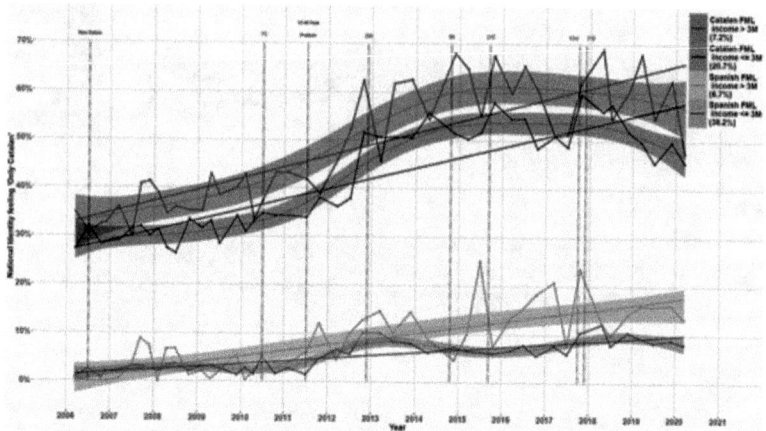

Figure 8.10 Evolution of feelings of "only Catalan" national identity depending on family/mother language and household net income (2006-2020). *Source*: Elaborated from CEO-Barometers survey microdata. Attached to each label are the population percentages for each group as of March 2020 survey. FML: Family-Mother Language. M=1000 Euros/month. Two top segment lines: family language Catalan; bottom segment lines: family language Spanish.

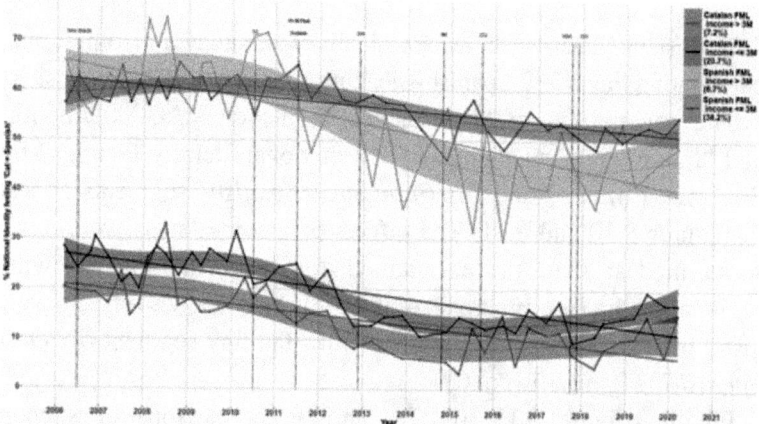

Figure 8.11 Evolution of feelings of "as Catalan as Spanish" national identity depending on family language and net household income (2006-2020). *Source*: Elaborated from CEO-Barometer survey microdata. Attached to each label are the population percentages for each group as of March 2020 survey. FML: Family-Mother Language. M= 1000 Euros/month. Two top segment lines: family language Spanish; bottom segment lines: family language Catalan.

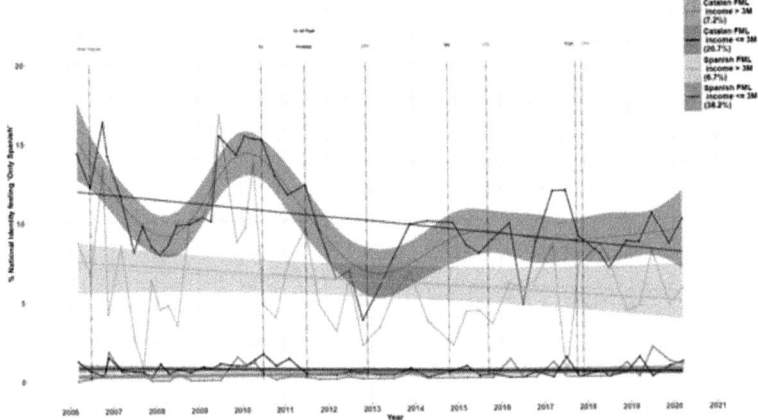

Figure 8.12 Evolution of feelings of "only Spanish" national identity depending on family language and net household income (2006-2020). *Source*: Elaborated from CEO-Barometer survey microdata. Observe the more intense oscillations within the FML Spanish segment (green). Observe also that the wealthier households that use the Spanish language reported less polarised feelings of national identity, the opposite than the equivalent Catalan language households (Figure 8.10). Attached to each label is the population percentages of each group in the March 2020 survey. FML: Family-Mother Language. M= 1000 Euros/month. Two gross segment lines: family language Spanish.

resources were much more in favour of secession. A very similar trend appeared when the perception of the evolution of one's own economic situation during the last year was measured. When that perception improved, support for secession was correspondingly higher. In all, these findings consistently indicate that the recent secessionist wave in Catalonia has been sustained by those segments within society that enjoy better economic resources and higher levels of well-being.

Taken together, therefore, all these findings indicate, in a solid way, that the recent secessionist venture in Catalonia was encouraged and maintained by the social segments that enjoy better economic resources and greater financial security. In other words, large well-established sectors of Catalan society have been the protagonists of this enduring and stubborn segregation movement, representing a group of 'privileged rebels', of sorts (35, 92, 96).

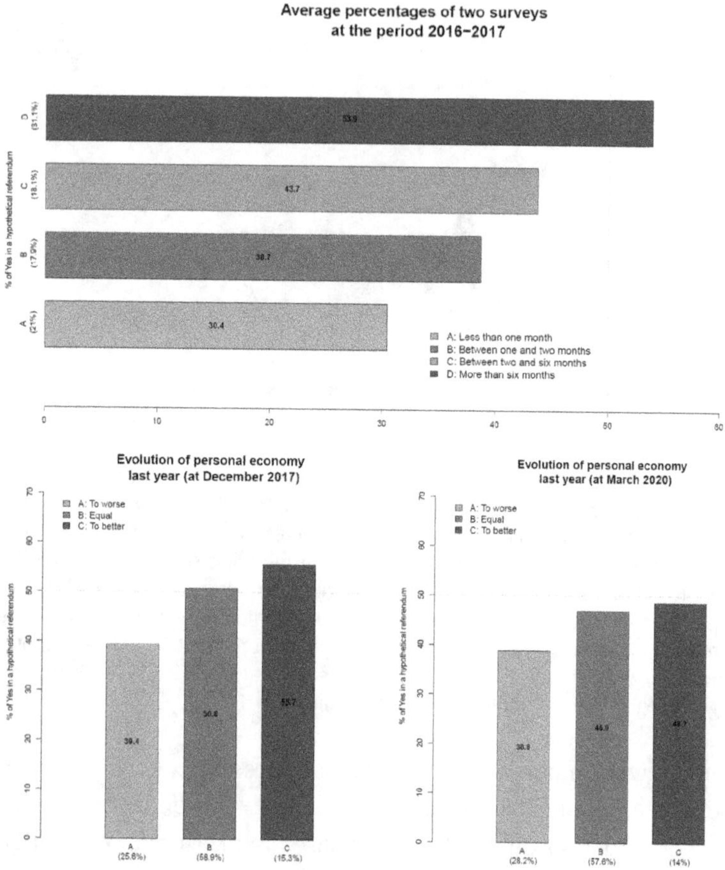

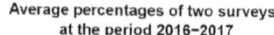

Figure 8.13 Support for secession and economic wellbeing. Top: Secession was much more popular among those with higher economic resistance limits (in months), in cases of economic breakdown. Bottom left: Secession was also more popular among those with a good perception of the evolution of their personal economic situation at the end of 2017. Bottom right: The same variable shows a bit less support for secession in spring 2020 (elaborated from CEO Barometer surveys).

To close this longitudinal description, Figure 8.14 (p. 71) displays the evolution of an estimate of the median levels of ideological self-perception between the extreme left (1) and extreme right (7) of each citizen, on a left to right scale (1 to 7 points), in population segments FML Catalan (black) and FML Spanish (gray). Note a

LONGITUDINAL PROFILES OF CATALONIAN CITIZENRY

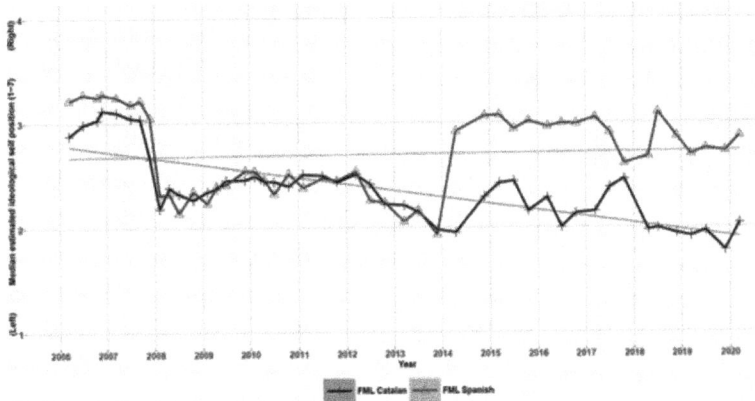

Figure 8.14 Evolution of median estimates of ideological self-position from 1 (Extreme Left) to 7 (Extreme Right) among citizens with family/mother language Catalan (black) vs those with family/mother language is Spanish (gray). Observe the differences between these groups and the clear change presented by citizens with family-mother language Spanish in 2014, when the first illegal independence referendum was organised by the regional government (CEO Barometers 2006–2020). FML: Family/mother language (FML Spanish: 56 per cent of the Catalonian citizenry; FML Catalan: 36 per cent; FML both Catalan and Spanish 6 per cent; *Source*: EULP2018-Enquesta Usos lingüístics de la població, Institut Estadístic Catalunya; (https:// www.idescat.cat/pub/?id=eulp).

shift to the left in both groups took place during the height of the economic crisis (2008-2012) and an abrupt growth to the right of FML Spanish-group followed in 2014, the date of the first illegal 'self-determination referendum' that had been sponsored by the regional government. Seemingly, the left parties played a permissive role with pro-secessionist forces leading the regional government.

IMPORTANT "BREAKING POINTS"

The longitudinal plots shown at Figures 8.2 through 8.6 contain several hallmarks signalling important dates from the recent secessionist campaign. Two recognisable "breaking points" flag the clearest departures towards distinctive polarisation profiles among the main segments of the Catalan citizenry. The first one appeared months before the ruling of the Spanish High Court in 2010 that modified the Statute of Autonomy (Home Rule), that had been approved in 2006. A second and much more important one was the decision taken by the moderate Nationalist Party that had been leading the regional government, for decades, to adopt a secessionist agenda around Autumn 2012. The prestigious hispanist Sir John Elliot (39) identified the same "breaking points" in his comparative account of the histories of Scotland and Catalonia, when he contrasted the lawful and negotiated Scottish bid for independence (preceding the independence referendum in 2014), with the unlawful and unilateral action in Catalonia (Autumn 2017).

The appearance of the first "breaking point" contradicts the usual depiction of the secessionist surge as a reaction of outrage against the "deep grievance" with the ruling of the Spanish High Court, that modified several articles of the region's new statute of autonomy in 2006 that had been approved by a minority of citizens; specifically, on a turnout of 48.85 percent (or 36 percent of the population) 73.24 percent were in favour of the new Statute, while 20.57 percent were against. Notably though, pro-secession preferences were already on the rise within an important fraction of the citizenry months before the court's decision. This is compatible with the proposal that the impact of the High Court decisions regarding home rule was truly influential, mainly because it was used as a political weapon to invigorate secessionist force and activism.

However, much more decisive was the period in the run-up to the regional elections of 25 November 2012. In fact, these elections marked the definitive point of departure for the secessionist wave, when the Catalonian President at that time, Artur Mas, leading a moderate nationalist party, lost his majority in the autonomous parliament. From that moment onwards, any parliamentary majority depended on various secessionist forces and the regional government then gradually opted for secession from Spain as its dominant strategy (9, 10, 39), Figures 8.2 and 8.4 illustrate how, around these elections, a segment of the citizenry (formed mainly of those with family/mother language Catalan) departed from a previous slowly rising tendency, towards an abrupt acceleration of reporting *"only Catalan"*, as their national identity. These percentages peaked around the first (illegal) consultation on secession (on 9 November 2014), and the growth stabilised at high levels as the struggle between the regional and Spanish central powers that persists today took form.

This population segment displayed parallel and consistent trends along several measures, including: feelings of national identity ("sense of belonging"); preferences for political links with Spain (i.e. opting for "independence"); and feelings of support for secession in a hypothetical (and legal) self-determination referendum. Such a narrowing of national self-identification linked to preferences for secession showed mainly by this group of "Catalan-natives", was not mirrored in the other big segments of the Catalonian citizenry (i.e. those with either Spanish or both Catalan and Spanish as their family/mother language). These segments tended to maintain a remarkable stability on their dual *"CatSpanish"* national identities without noticeable changes.

PARTISAN CLASHES WITHIN A DIVIDED SOCIETY

The supporters of Catalonian independence attempted, initially at least, to present itself as a peaceful and socially inclusive movement that wanted to reach and fulfil its ultimate political objective through unambiguously democratic means. The frequent, enormous and usually festive street demonstrations claiming the "right to vote" in a referendum on independence underscored and consolidated this perception for years. The fierce political struggle between the static Spanish powers and the much more dynamic regional administration also contributed to disseminate that view among many observers (31, 32, 38, 50, 80, 82).

This changed dramatically when regional powers announced, at the start of summer 2017, that they were going to call for a binding referendum despite repeated warnings by the Spanish High Court that this would violate constitutional law. Nonetheless a referendum was planned that would be followed by segregation from Spain in the case of a simple majority victory. Nonetheless, the supporters of independence persevered (see "Situation map" depiction, p2), which had the effect of awakening the response of the unionist citizenry (who represent around three million people, from an electoral census (i.e. total number of eligible voters) of 5.5 million, within a population of more than 7 million). Catalan unionists had remained mostly silent and expectant throughout the secessionist surge, but during the weeks preceding the "independence declaration" (which took place on 27 October 2017), there was a marked and recorded rise in unionist activism, reflected in the enormous unionist rally that was held on 8 October in Barcelona (Figure 8.15, 8.16) amid the escalating tensions that pervaded all scenarios (10, 44, 64, 80, 82, 101).

Such tensions have taken many forms over the last years, mainly through low-intensity street clashes and manifestations related to attempts to monopolise public places with secessionist symbols and

Figure 8.15 Unionists were able to deploy massive street demonstrations in downtown Barcelona. *Source*: La Vanguardia, Google Images.

Figure 8.16 One of the gigantic demonstrations that secessionists repeatedly mounted. This rallie and the one depicted at Figure 8.15, were separated by less than a month on autumn 2017. Source: La Vanguardia. Google Images.

to mount protests against the trial of rebellious leaders who were in prison or exile (10, 44, 80, 82). The protests against the sentence of the Supreme Court that had condemned the rebel leaders in prison took on a particularly high intensity, including acts of serious vandalism, in the autumn of 2019. The riots managed to put the joint action of the Catalan and Spanish Police forces in check for two weeks and resulted in a multitude of wounded and detained people, which was in addition to serious damage that had been caused to private and public assets in various cities (93).

However, the main and unavoidable legacy of the failed secessionist attempt has been the deepening divisions within a society that had been presented, for decades, as a model of porosity and conviviality. This division runs essentially through an unsealed ethnolinguistic cleavage with accompanying economic differences which were previously attenuated through the myriad interactions that a truly open and contemporary society can offer.

There have been repeated but unsuccessful attempts to deny the conflictive division and the affective fracture within Catalonian society. These attempts have included a wide range of initiatives: from "diplomacy" actions by delegates of the regional government all over the world, to persistent media campaigns and scholarship in support of secession (123). The main message of these actions is that Catalonia is a multi-hybrid and encompassing society containing a rich variety of communities with very different interests. Of course, most societies are hybrid and contain nuanced complexities, but they can still be strongly and acutely polarised around a single and important political issue, as is the case in Catalonia (21, 74, 75, 122).

PROVISIONAL CONCLUSIONS

Globally, this series of longitudinal findings has confirmed the notable polarisation that exists in Catalonia around the issue of secession that others had previously shown based on a handful of surveys and electoral results. Moreover, the findings presented here highlight the important covariations that exist between the outstanding changes to feelings of national identity throughout the secessionist push, by examining: whether family/mother language was Catalan or Spanish; preference for regional of other media, and differences regarding economic and personal well-being. The scope of statistical associations deployed here are far from trivial and deserve serious attention.

Concerning the first one, before the dawn of the secessionist surge Miley (77, 78) had already established the existence of divergent national identities in the main segments of Catalan society that broke down along an ethnolinguistic frontier. Departing from CIS surveys and other social data, Miley challenged the depiction of the Catalonian bid for sovereignty as a form of "civic nationalism." He highlighted the operation of an ethnolinguistic cleavage that distinguished between two population fractions, with "native, Catalan-speaking" citizens on one side and their Spanish-speaking neighbours with immigrant origins, at the other. "Mother tongue" had, in fact, the strongest impact upon an individual's self-recognition as predominantly Catalan as opposed to expressing predominantly Spanish or mixed "*CatSpanish*" identities. In subsequent studies, he showed that there was a notorious gap between the preferences of citizens and options preferred by their representatives, as the language policy implemented by the regional powers was inconsistent with the preferences of Spanish-speaking citizens. He identified, moreover, two mechanisms that blocked their representation in the region's institutions: first, a clear under-representation of those citizens in autonomous powers; and second, a partial assimilation of some Spanish-speaking elected politicians into the attitudes of Catalan-speaking rulers.

He concluded that the social bases of support for Catalan nationalism were "overwhelmingly ethnic" and that the separatist movement was an elite-led, "top down" project. The present series of findings offer strong support for these conclusions by showing that segmentation across the ethnolinguistic divide was crucially linked to distinctive polarisation profiles during the whole period of the secessionist surge. Hurried attempts to disguise this reality (123) by claiming that both the iterated discourses and political actions of all secessionist forces have always been inclusive, could not hide the strong segmentation of citizens' preferences across the aforementioned ethno-linguistic frontier.

The divergent and increasingly polarised identities were also associated, to an important degree, with differential exposure to the media under direct or indirect control of the regional powers. Following the regional public media or not was an important mediator of the changes in feelings of national identity and of preferences for secession. The strong gaps in media following preferences (for news and political debates) based essentially on family-language divisions, surely contributed to an exaggeration of the distinctive communal attachments and frames of reference on both sides of the ethnolinguistic frontier: Catalans or *CatSpanish*. TV channels, newspapers and other broadcasting outlets, which are directly or indirectly under the control of the regional government, not only dominated but fully encapsulated the secessionist audiences operating only or mostly, in the Catalan language. This represents an obvious mismatch as Spanish is the language of daily use of more than half of Catalonian citizens[4]. This reflects the operation of a "communication bubble" that nourished the secessionist fraction, as middle class natives and assimilated citizens who use Catalan language almost exclusively get their political opinion mainly from local media (10, 26, 31, 77, 78, 118, 119, 120). Despite unresolved discussions regarding the power of media to modify social opinion, there is widespread agreement on their important influence over segmented audiences (98, 99, 112).

Social networks have also been an important vector for the rising segmentation of attachments and affects inside the unionist and secessionist cohorts, though there is ongoing discussion about its relative relevance (98, 99, 112). A large-scale analysis provided solid evidence that during the 2017 illegal "referendum" for Catalonian independence, social media bots generated and promoted violent content, aimed mainly at the secessionist population segment (116). Nearly 4 million Twitter posts, on that issue alone, generated by almost 1 million users, were monitored and analysed over two weeks around the event. The findings clearly indicate that automated social media content contributed to an exacerbation of the serious political conflict.

During deep political crises, the existence of unsealed ethnocultural cleavages is a widely known pre-requisite for the triggering of quick polarisation and partisanship alignments between and within neighboring communities (1, 40, 41, 58, 81). The divide in Catalonia has not spilled into an open violent conflict, though tensions were high especially in autumn 2017 and they still subsist, though in attenuated form, while the situation remains at a chronic standstill. All kind of frictions appear nowadays in different social scenarios and contribute to the confrontation between these two communities who had enjoyed a long tradition of tolerant and convivial coexistence. There have been worries that such a divide could lead to intergroup clashes that would carry the ingredients that appear in other societies that shelter unsealed ethno-cultural frontiers (40, 41, 48, 58, 65, 81, 101, 113, 115). The riots and guerrilla actions following the sentences handed down by the Supreme Court in October 2019 provide an idea of what could emerge on a wider scale in the event of a sustained and unresolved conflict in the region (93, 95).

The highest achievement of the Catalonian secessionist venture has been the creation of an intense devotion for the goal of attaining full sovereignty, as an independent state, to the point of carrying the traits of a collective romantic passion that engages an impressive segment of the Catalonian citizenry. However, such passion hardly entices the rest of Catalan population. The in-group self-glorification ingredients conveyed by such nationalistic passion excluded, by definition, other communities within the region (23, 118, 120).

The secessionist movement has been persistently nourished by partisan autonomous powers, responding, most likely, to the tenacious litigation between various secessionist forces to lead the regional administration (9, 10, 29, 118, 122). The series of findings presented in this chapter have unveiled important operating tracks of a top-down induced civil conflict that has left, as its main legacy, a deeply divided community within a fully open and democratic society at the heart of Europe.

IMMERSIVE EDUCATION
Another Divisive Tool

The longitudinal findings discussed so far established family/mother language—either Spanish or Catalan languages—as the essential feature that best describes the division created by the secessionist push. Such linguistic distinction was much more important than economic variations or the biased influence of partisan media controlled by the secessionist regional administration.

The amiable conviviality between the Catalan and Spanish language communities—not so distant indeed, as both languages are derived from old Latin—is an undeniable fact in all areas of daily live in the region. Easy and cordial coexistence, however, does not erase an unavoidable form of competition as always happen with societies that have more than one official language. Political intervention into school programmes has been one of the areas of most frequent discrepancy and ceaseless discussions, especially regarding the relevance and differentiated roles that the Catalan and Spanish languages are afforded.

EDUCATION AND NATIONAL-IDENTITY: CATALONIAN "*IMMERSIVE SCHOOLING*"

Catalan language evolved from Latin on both sides of the Eastern part of the Pyrenées, between the tenth and eleventh centuries. It was initially confined to the valleys across these high mountains, but from late thirteenth century it followed the expansion of the Aragon Kingdom southwards, along the Mediterranean coastline of the Iberian Peninsula, and going further still, even to some parts of Sardinia and Sicily. Nowadays it's commonly spoken in both Spanish and French Catalonia, in other Spanish regions such as Valencia and in the Balearic Islands, and also in Andorra (the only official language there), and in a single tiny Sardinian county. It is currently spoken by almost 10 million people, making it one of the most extended regional languages in Europe. Spanish Catalonia is the area that hosts the greatest number of this group, with around 7 million speakers.

After the formation of Spain in the fifteenth century, the Catalan language remained mostly a familial/domestic tongue for a number of centuries and only entered into formal education in a handful of primary schools at the end of nineteenth century, in the context of a "*Renaixença*" (rebirth) of Catalan culture. This political and social movement successfully promoted the use of, and instruction in, Catalan language during the first half of the twentieth century and, particularly, along during the life of the Second Spanish Republic (1931-1939), when a wide network of Catalan schools was created across the region. After the Spanish Civil war (1936-1939), such initiatives were dismantled and all formal education was delivered uniquely in Spanish language, until the end of the authoritarian regime that followed (1939-1975). From the second half of the sixties, however, there were efforts to reintroduce Catalan language in some primary schools and its domestic use had spread already into many professional areas. Once the military dictatorship ended (1975), Spain quickly transformed itself into an open and largely decentralised country: regions received wide capacities for self-government through specific home rule provisions and were allowed to legislate through their own regional parliaments. This opportunity was used to bring the Catalan language into a prevalent position within society.

A highly influential law issued by the Catalonian regional parliament was the '*Language Normalisation Act*' (LNA, 1983), whose main goal was to promote the use of the Catalan language in all professional and private settings. The law thus sought to provide the tools for the educational system to establish a fully bilingual society. Although schools had been teaching Catalan language as an ordinary subject since 1978, it was not recognised as a main language for education until 1983. All students, irrespective of their origin, were supposed to efficiently use both Catalan and Spanish languages at the end of their education, and the *Certificate of Basic Educational Attainment* could not be obtained without proving proficiency in both. The law promoted, in fact, the adoption of an "*immersive system*" by establishing that students should not be allocated into different classes because of their distinct familial language, and that Catalan language had to be introduced with precedence as the first or the main language throughout the school curriculum, while Spanish language should follow as the second official language. The law was applicable to all education levels including pre-school, primary and secondary levels. This was consolidated in 1998 with a *Language Policy Law* (LPL). At universities, language use was left to the preference of lecturers and instructors, although specific plans to increase the use of Catalan language were also introduced across the higher education sector.

Like other educational reforms, the introduction of *immersive bilingualism* in Catalan schools was associated with other adjustments. A direct implication of the new linguistic policy was the adoption of textbooks and teaching materials written in the Catalan language. The contents of courses were also modified: Catalonian culture, history and geography had to be taught, in parallel with Spanish culture. The reform did not involve, however, a replacement of the teaching staff and thousands of teachers benefited from swift training schemes in the Catalan language. Catalan language knowledge tests were introduced during the recruitment of new teachers and became compulsory in 1989:[1] those who failed had to commit to becoming proficient in Catalan language within a few years of qualifying.

In 1994 the Spanish Constitutional Court acknowledged the validity of the '*immersive model*' for primary and pre-schooling education, with Catalan as the main language of instruction, while Spanish remained compulsory but limited to language courses and a minimum number of subjects were taught in Spanish (5-10 percent of instruction time at primary education (45)). Language use in secondary schools was less affected by changes introduced by the Language Normalisation Act, but the subsequent *Language Policy Law* (LPL) of 1998 established the "*immersive regime*" as mandatory in all non-University education, at least in public schools. LPL also implemented several changes regarding the relevance of Catalan language in the labour market. First, it established a required level of proficiency in Catalan language as a prerequisite for entering public sector employment. Second, it incentivised the use of Catalan language in private business, especially among firms who had links with the regional public sector, and service firms with a strong contact with customers.

The transition towards a school system in which Catalan was the main language did not result, apparently, in less proficiency in Spanish language, however. Centralised tests by Spanish and Catalan education authorities indicated that at the end of compulsory schooling the level of proficiency in both languages were similar, and Spanish language skills of Catalonian students were not different from averages across Spain (45, 125).

In a series of studies, Irma Clots-Figueras and associates (5, 6, 24) presented pioneering findings that showed that the introduction of Catalonian educational reforms in 1983 moved both national identity and political preferences towards higher levels of self-identification linked to nation-building goals. Using a 2001 CIS survey where a representative sample of more than 2.300 citizens from different age cohorts were interviewed, they demonstrated on the five-level scale of "*feelings of belonging*" (see p. 41), that "*Catalan only*" or "*more Catalan than Spanish*" self-identities correlated positively with the

IMMERSIVE EDUCATION

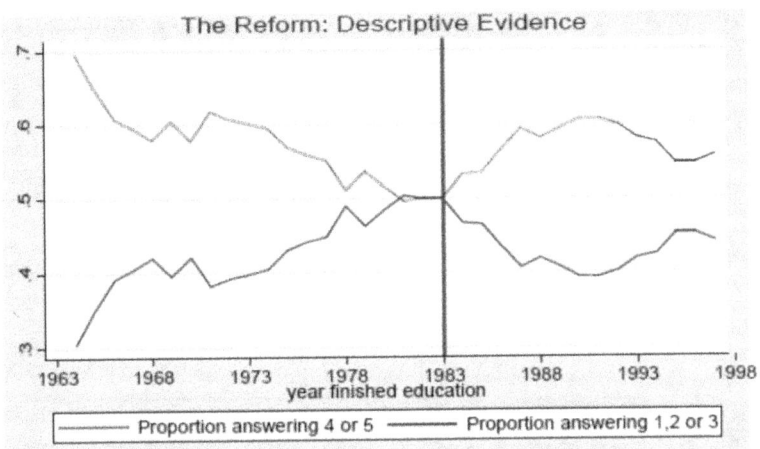

Figure 9.1 Proportions of people answering that they felt "Only Catalan" (4) and "More Catalan than Spanish" (5) versus the rest (1, 2 and 3), plotted along the years that they finished education*. *Note*: *(1= "I feel only Spanish"; 2= "I feel More Spanish than Catalan"; 3= "I feel as Catalan as Spanish"). Reproduced with permission from (6).

number of years of education received under the new Catalan language *"immersive instruction"* regime in schools (see Figures 9.2 and 9.3, for a summary).

A similar trend appeared when the authors considered measures of political preferences, detecting an increasing electoral support for nationalist parties and a higher approval for the right of self-determination for Catalonia (Figure 9.8, p. 96). The influence of the new educational framework was clearly higher for those individuals whose parents were born in Catalonia, but was also noticeable for those whose parents were born outside the region.

Figure 9.1 shows that once the relevant Constitutional and home rule provisions were approved, there were six years (1978-1983) of almost perfect stability regarding national identities: they were equally distributed between preferences for either "Catalonian" or "Spanish" self-identification feelings. However, after the introduction of the educational reform of 1983 that was designed to promote a dominant role for Catalan language in schools, the lines started

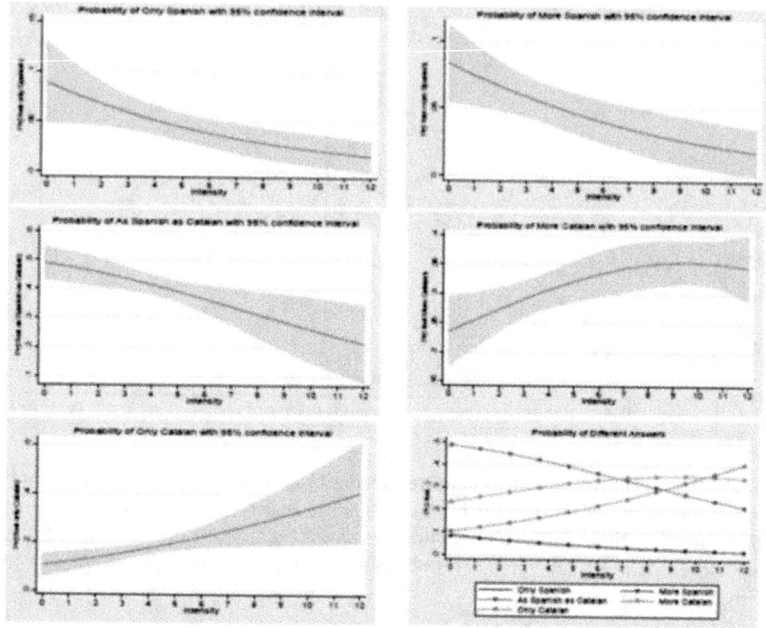

Figure 9.2 Change in probabilities for the five "national identity" categories, depending on the instruction intensity. Intensity = years of education received under the 1983 "Immersive law" promoting prominence for Catalan language at schools. Adapted with permission from (6).

to diverge towards a systematic increase in *"Catalonian-biased"* national identity and a parallel decrease in rates of *"Spanish-biased"* national identity.

Figure 9.2 sets out these changes for the different "national identities" by illustrating the probability of variation due to the influence of such educational reform. The authors estimated that every year of exposure to the reform increased the probability of feeling *"only Catalan"*, *"more Catalan than Spanish"* or *"as Catalan as Spanish"* by more than 2 percentage points.

The authors introduced several internal controls to discard potential confounding effects due to certain characteristics of the cohorts, including: levels of educational attainment, provincial attachment, gender, family descent, migration, social use of language and

IMMERSIVE EDUCATION

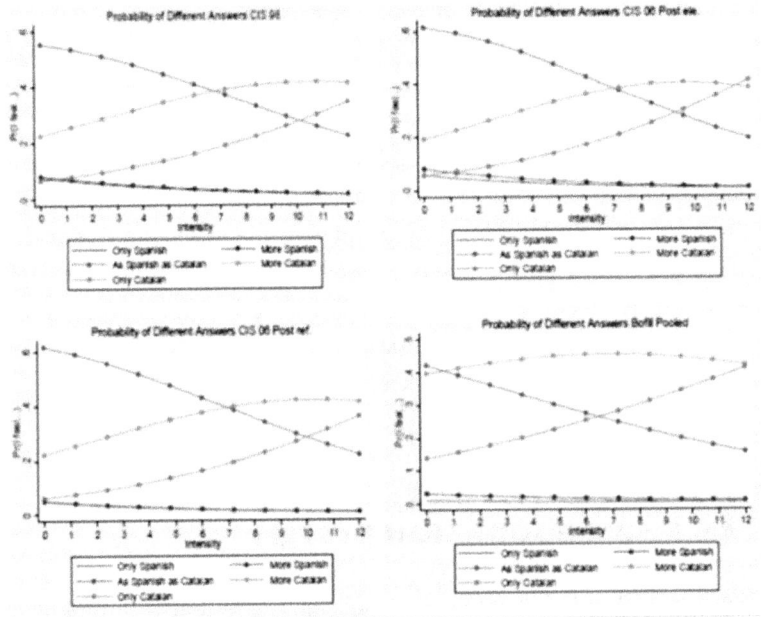

Figure 9.3 Change probabilities for five "national identity" categories, depending on the instruction intensity. Intensity = years of education under the 1983 "Immersive law", promoting prominence for Catalan language at schools. Findings from different surveys: CIS 1998, 2005, 2006 and Bofill Foundation (2001-2005). Results fully confirm those depicted at Figure 9.1, from CIS 2001 survey. Adapted with permission from (6).

several other factors. They also compared their data with those from another CIS 2001 survey completed, at the same time, in the Basque Country. In that Spanish region families can select whether they prefer a formal education for their children in *Euskera* (Basque language) or in Spanish language, as the main language of instruction, or through a mixed model. Thus, schools can use separate language regimes across the curriculum. Notably, there were no effects of the intensity of instruction (years of education received) on national identity or political preferences in the Basque country. Hence, the authors conclude that the nation-building biased/directional effects of the Catalonian education system, based on a compulsory predominance of Catalan language, was probably causal, and the immersive system with Catalan as the main educational language was causing a bias towards a stronger national self-identification as Catalan-only (5, 6, 24).

These studies are important because they showed that an education system can have noticeable effects on feelings and perceptions relating to nation-building, by changing identities and political preferences, from very early on after being implemented. Though the effects detected between 2001–2006 were smaller than the ones described here for the period 2006–2019, the underlying tendencies were already there, as we shall see.

GAPS INDUCED BY CATALONIAN "IMMERSIVE EDUCATION SYSTEM"

Calero and Choi (16) launched a study into the effects of immersive policies in Catalonia, focusing on the academic performance of students. They wanted to fill a curious absence of empirical evidence regarding this issue. According to them there were two reasons to explain this void: first, the lack of variation in Catalonian educational policy precluded the gathering of proper control groups to carry out robust contrasts; second, usual assessments of academic performance at the regional and national levels have limitations that hinder the analysis of the effects of different policies.

The authors used data from the 2015 wave of PISA (*Programme for International Student Assessment* that looks at OECD countries), which evaluated the performance of 15-year-old Catalonian students into the test administered in Catalan language, as well as the student's abilities in reading, science and maths. The full sample involved 52 centres (including both public and "subsidised" private centers within the auspices of the regional administration), with a total of 1,769 students being evaluated. This excluded the fully private (non-subsidised) centres, because not all of them apply the immersion schooling in Catalan language. In order to ensure that the students analysed received identical treatment (i.e. language immersion throughout all years of compulsory schooling), those students who declared having arrived in Spain at 6 years of age or older were also excluded from the sample. After these two filters, the final sample totalled 1,347 students, equally divided for gender, enrolled across 44 centres.

Figure 9.4 and Table 9.1 depict the direct comparisons on scores of these three areas of academic performance—science, reading, maths—depending on the language usually spoken at home (i.e. family/mother language).

A quick inspection of Figure 9.4 suggest a strong detrimental effect on PISA scores of coming from homes where the family/mother language is not Catalan. Such diminished performance was noticeable for students from Spanish language homes and even more so for students coming from homes speaking another language (the majority, from migrant homes). The language of the PISA test (Catalan version) could partially explain these differences, but other comparisons listed in Table 9.1 also indicate that other factors also

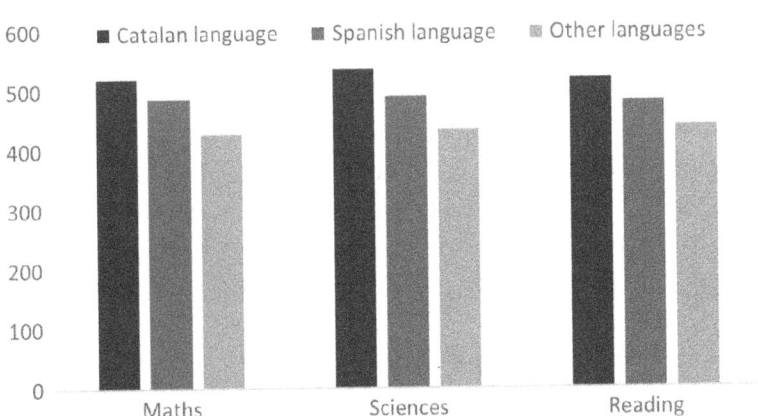

Figure 9.4 **Academic performance in different cognitive skills – maths, science, reading – of Catalonian students (15 years old), as assessed by PISA-2015 test wave, depending on Family/Mother Language.** Modified from (16). Black-gray gradations indicate Family-Mother Languages of the students tested.

Table 9.1 Sciences competences (PISA) of 15 years old Catalonian students depending on family language, sex, test centre, region and socioeconomic/cultural background*

	Family-Mother Language			Diff. Cat-Spanish	Diff. Cat-Other
	Catalan	Spanish	Other		
SEX					
Boys	537.35	494.75	422.25	42.6	115,1
Girls	520.9	486.79	440.69	34.11	80.21
Difference	16.45	7.96	18.44		
CENTER					
Public	528.04	483.22	427.02	44.82	101.02
Subsidized	534.61	515.33	495.95	19.28	38.66
Difference	-6.57	-32.11	-68.93		
SITE					
Barcelona	541.71	499.98	466.97	41.73	74.74
Rest of Catalonia	529.57	490.87	433.33	38.60	92.24
Difference	12.14	9.11	33.64		
SOCIOECONOMIC/CULTURAL LEVEL:					
33 per cent Higher	550.81	524.27	496.66	26.54	54.15
33 per cent Lower	490.57	474.83	414.81	15.74	75.76
Difference	60.24	49.44	81.85		

*Reproduced from 16.

contribute to this. Applying multilevel regression analyses to the sample as a whole, Calero and Choi (16) were able to confirm their initial conjecture that "*students who use Spanish language at home, being educated in an immersion regime in Catalan language, would achieve inferior performance in the competences evaluated by PISA, with respect to that of their classmates whose family language is Catalan, with independence of the rest of personal, socio-cultural and economic characteristics*". The observed contrasts fully confirm such hypothesis in the case of science and reading skills, but rejected it in math skills.

Students from homes that commonly speak Spanish got 10.85 points less at PISA assessment of scientific ability compared to students whose language at home was Catalan. The same comparison also gave 10.30 points less for reading abilities (Fig. 9.4). The lack of significance of the influence of family/mother language on mathematical ability can be explained by the fact that ability in maths requires a specific formalised language that presumably protected about the disadvantage of being educated and evaluated in a language that is different from the language spoken at home.

When analysing the influence of many other variables on the gap between students from distinct family/mother languages, several heterogeneities appear. A summary of the relevant effects on scientific abilities are set out in Table 9.2. Regarding sex, such contrasts were negative only for boys, while girls were unaffected. Concerning contrasts between centres, comparisons were negative for public centres, but not for subsidised ("concerted") centers. The municipality where students were resident was also relevant; with the exception of Barcelona, in all municipalities the contrasts indicated significantly worse results for students whose family/mother language was Spanish. Finally, when distinguishing according to the level of economic and socio-cultural status (SECS), differences appeared in the upper segment, but not in the lower one.

These results clearly point to the existence of an equity problem, which generates *"academic losers"* that can derive from the policy

Table 9.2 Summary of coefficients from hierarchical lineal regressions on several sub-samples on Catalonia PISA-2015 test, for sciences abilities (comparisons with Family-Mother Language Catalan)

	Family language Spanish	Family language Others
Girls	No significant difference	No significant difference
Boys	- 15.92**	- 34,36
Public School	- 11.91**	- 27,32**
Concerted School	No significant difference	No significant difference
Barcelona	No significant difference	No significant difference
Rest of Catalonia	- 11.62**	- 33.77**
33 per cent Higher SECS	- 22.9**	- 38.48**
33 per cent Lower SECS	No significant difference	No significant difference

*Modified from (16). ** p<.01. SECS: socio-economic cultural status.

of linguistic immersion in Catalonia. The findings indicate that the "immersion system" in schools has an undeniable problematic dimension that has not yet been sufficiently considered.

The iterated propagandistic presentation of the linguistic immersion system in Catalonia as an example of a very "successful policy", that promotes both social cohesion and opportunities for advancement in the job market and regarding earning potential (19), has therefore a component related to political nation-building goals. This propaganda lacks robust endorsement by a large enough body of empirical evidence (45, 125, 128). The findings of Calero and Choi (16) provide an important cautionary warning about non-trivial negative effects on the academic performance of students coming from homes where Catalan language is not the family language. It is also worth remembering that this includes the majority of households in the region.

CITIZENS PERCEPTION ON LINGUISTIC "IMMERSIVE SYSTEM", AT CATALONIAN SCHOOLS.

Garvía and Santana (45) provided the first large-scale survey into the opinions of the Catalonian citizenry regarding the "immersive regime" of language education in schools. Before this study, only a much less ambitious CIS-1998 survey had explored this issue that has so often been at the forefront of political debate.

Table 9.3 Preferences for linguistic regime in Catalonian school system in 1998*

Question: How do you think basic education should be conducted in Catalonia? CIS-2298 (1998). N= 1006.	
Everything in Spanish language	0,8 per cent
Most in Spanish and some in Catalan	4 per cent
Half and half	50,2 per cent
Most in Catalan and some in Spanish	33,2 per cent
Everything in Catalan language	9,3 per cent
No response	2,5 per cent

Note: *Modified from 45.

IMMERSIVE EDUCATION

Table 9.3 shows that the preferred option for most respondents, at that time, was an equal treatment of both Catalan and Spanish in schools.

Garvía and Santana (45) surveyed a representative sample of 2202 individuals (aged eighteen years and over) in 2016. The sample was stratified according to population size and strata in each one of the four Catalan provinces. Respondents were interviewed by phone and were selected by random digit dialling, considering the provincial distributions of age and gender. Interviewers were bilingual and interviewees could choose to answer either in Catalan or Spanish.

More than twenty years after the CIS-1998 survey, the profile of results was almost identical (Figure 9.5): the "immersive system" is approved by 50 percent of the citizenry, while there is another half of the population who would prefer a system that would allow parents to decide regarding school language or that would fix two

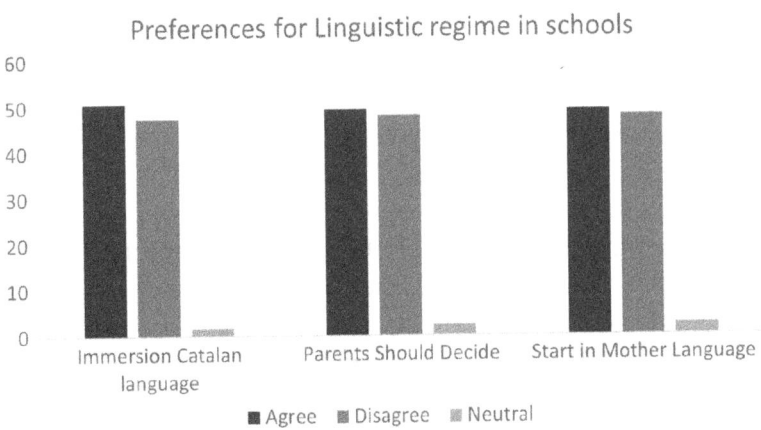

Figure 9.5 Preferences of Catalonian population regarding the linguistic regime in schools. N=2.202. Figures add up to 100 per cent. The "agree" category combines "strongly agree" and "agree", while the "disagree" category includes "disagree" and "strongly disagree". "Neutral" option (neither agree nor disagree), was not provided by interviewers to encourage respondents to take a position. (Modified from 45).

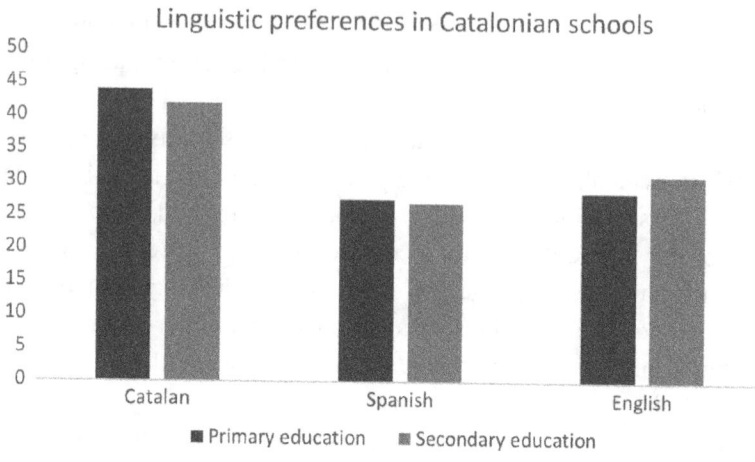

Figure 9.6 Preferences of Catalonian population regarding the linguistic regime in schools. N (Primary education) = 2.197; N (Secondary education) = 2.198. Figures add up to 100 per cent. (Modified from 45)

differentiated options according to family/mother language. Figure 9.7 shows that the opinions of the Catalonian citizenry are split and polarised depending again on family/mother language, with Catalan native speakers overwhelmingly preferring the "immersive system" (73 percent), whereas Spanish native speakers were mostly against it (63 percent). An equivalent polarization appeared when opinions regarding the *"immersive system"* were combined with political preferences regarding Catalonian secession from Spain (see Figure 9.8): those in favour of secession strongly approved of the "immersive system" (78 percent), whereas the non-secessionists were clearly against it (74 percent). This polarised split was moderated again when options included the views of parents or regarding the possibility of distinct educational distinctions according to family/mother languages.

When regarding the weight that English language should have in school, answers became more distributed (Figures 9.6, 9.9 and 9.10). All groups gave some precedence to Catalan language and similar percentages were recorded for Spanish and English, although Catalan native speakers expressed a marked preference for Catalan

IMMERSIVE EDUCATION

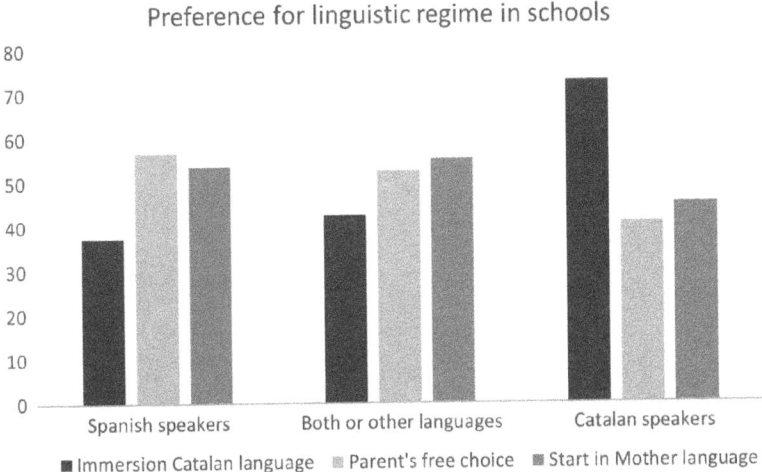

Figure 9.7 Preferences regarding the linguistic regime in schools, by family/ mother tongue: percentage of agreement. Immersion N = 2.097, Free Choice N= 2.083 and Start in Mother tongue N=2.084. Percentages reporting neither agree nor disagree were: 1.8, 2.4 and 2.5, respectively; χ^2 = 249.2 (p<0.001), 47.5 (p<0.001) and 15.1 (p<0.001), for the three contrasts. See previous figure 9.5 for details on the coding of "agree" and "disagree" categories. Modified from 45.

language and placed less emphasis on English and Spanish (see Figures 9.9 and 9.10).

Garvía and Aranda (45) summarized these findings emphasising the following points:

1. *Only half of the Catalonian citizenry support the current linguistic immersion policy, believing that "All children should have their primary education entirely in Catalan language".*
2. *Support for linguistic immersion, however, is significantly stronger among the political elite, which suggests a gulf between the preferences of politicians and their constituents.*
3. *A similar proportion of Catalonian citizens approve of clear alternative policies that endorse individual linguistic rights.*
4. *When interviewees were asked to express their preferences not in terms of linguistic rights but rather in terms of the distribution*

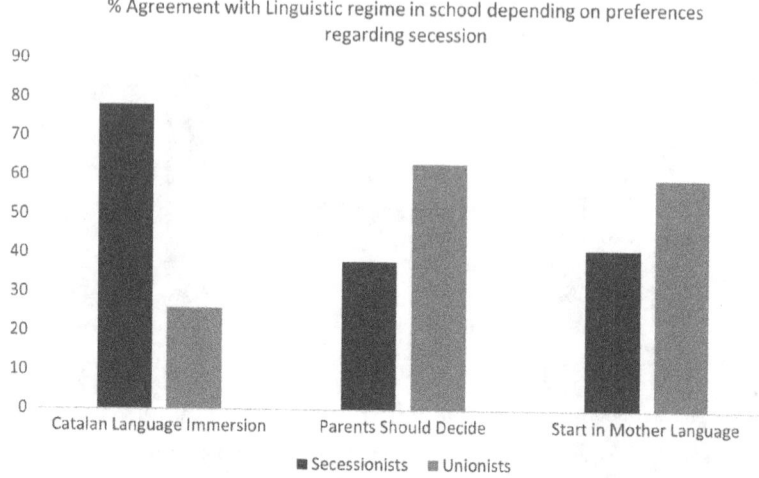

Figure 9.8 Preferences for linguistic regime in schools depending on preferences regarding secession. Percentage of agreement (per cent disagreement: remnants up to 100) Immersion question N = 1.993; χ2 = 541.7 (p<0.001); Free Choice N = 1.978; χ2 = 125.0 (p<0.001). Mother language N = 1.979, χ2 = 65.0 (p<0.001). Percentages for neither agree nor disagree were 1.7, 2.4 and 2.3, respectively. Modified from 45.

of teaching hours, the average distribution preference gives less weight to the Catalan language than to the current linguistic immersion system.

5. *Although there is a clear divide between native Catalan and Spanish speakers regarding their preferences regarding the linguistic regime, when these preferences are expressed quantitatively (in terms of the desired distribution of teaching hours in each language), the divide is not so deep. Both groups, it turns out, agreed to prioritise Catalan language about other languages in education.*

6. *Most individuals agreed that an ultimately independent Catalonia should not have Catalan language as the only official language.*

7. *Even the minority of Catalonians who would like Catalonia to be an independent state with Catalan language as its sole*

IMMERSIVE EDUCATION

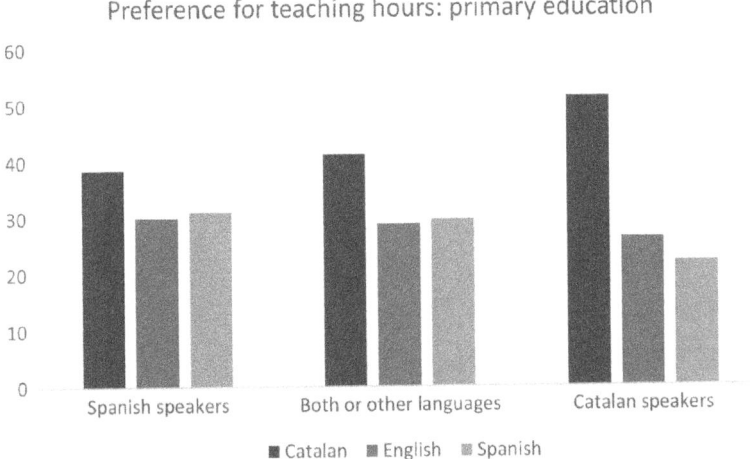

Figure 9.9 Preferences for distribution of teaching hours for Catalan, Spanish and English language courses. N = 2.130 (Primary education), 2.131 (Secondary education). Percentages of teaching time preferred for each language (i.e. for each group of native speakers). "Both or other" includes Catalonian and Spanish native bilinguals plus native speakers of other languages. Differences between Catalan and Spanish native speakers; and between Catalan speakers and "Both or other" were statistically significant; differences between Spanish speakers and "Both or other" were not. Modified from 45.

official language, would like Spanish language to have more weight in the school system than the current linguistic immersion policy dictates.

8. The demand for English, measured in terms of teaching hours, is slightly lower than that for Catalan and Spanish. This demand is lower among Catalan native speakers and Catalans with pro-secession sentiments than among Spanish native speakers and Catalonians who oppose secession.

The authors concluded by asserting that:

Given these results, should we conclude that the divide between the two linguistic communities in Catalonia and the current political polarisation between pro- and anti-secession factions make it

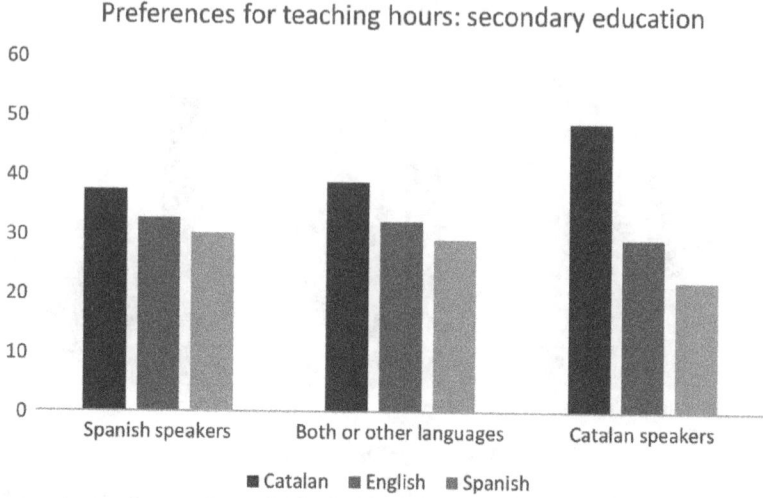

Figure 9.10 Preferences for distribution of teaching hours for Catalan, Spanish and English language courses. N = 2.130 (Primary education), 2.131 (Secondary education). Percentages of teaching time preferred for each language (i.e. for each group of native speakers). "Both or other" includes Catalonian and Spanish native bilinguals plus native speakers of other languages. Differences between Catalan and Spanish native speakers; and between Catalan speakers and "Both or other" were statistically significant; differences between Spanish speakers and "Both or other" were not. Modified from 45.

impossible to adapt a linguistic regime to satisfy all parties? Probably not if it is emphasised 1) that there is ground for agreement among Catalonians regarding this contested issue—particularly when focusing on responses regarding the language distribution of teaching hours; and 2) that this common ground could be enlarged were both Catalan and Spanish political elites more willing to accept the value of multilingualism and stop using languages as political tools of competing national projects.

This is prudent and sound advice, although it appears a bit detached given the degree of polarisation within Catalonian society. In fact, educational policy has been a preferred field for partisan action. The issues that have predominated have been a biased and systematic education policy from the regional pro-secession administration against the preferences of a majority of the Catalonian citizenry and an outstanding and curious absence of action by the central Spanish administration.

In light of the findings presented in this chapter and the important cautions related to basic individual and family rights that have been discussed (30, 109, 125, 128), it seems advisable to rethink the ways that the current linguistic policy in Catalonia is conceived of and applied.

A DANGEROUS DECADE (2010-2020)

Over the past ten years, a good portion of the Catalonian citizenry had the privilege of living through a sensational political adventure that could be seen as unique, in the annals of European democracies. The setting-up a popular movement of enormous force and dynamism, directed to achieve the neatly defined target of segregation from Spain, and arriving at the threshold of achieving its ultimate goal, is an indisputable achievement and a memorable milestone that will no doubt endure not only in the memories of those who contributed to this venture, but also among those who witnessed it first-hand (82, 84, 107, 118).

However, as this extraordinary campaign did not achieve its ultimate goal the seriousness of the secessionist challenge is now typically diminished by many analysts. The strategic skills of the secessionist leadership that led Catalonian society through this unprecedent period have also been highly criticised. What's more, several prominent secessionist leaders have also suffered exile or imprisonment[1].

It is my considered opinion that this swift description of the panorama, now that the heat has gone from the secessionist battle is, in fact, wrong. I suspect this because the issue did not end with a flagrant defeat of the secessionists and not even with a narrow loss, but with a draw. This tie was sealed when a new autonomous government with a secessionist majority was formed in mid-2018, which has sustained the impasse and has kept the region bogged-down (politically speaking) ever since. This is not a complete fiasco, but a chronic and entrenched tie that is generating many skirmishes and much tension that fails to clear the air one way or another.

One of the most common ways to dilute the seriousness of the secessionist bid, is to endorse the "bluff conjecture" that the former regional government minister, Clara Ponsatí, made explicit from her Scottish exile. The most entertaining chronicle of this apparent bluff can be found in "*57 days on Piolín*", the meticulous, skeptical and affable diary that Guillem Martínez published *online* with commendable dedication (71). This chronicle began, in fact, with an explicit prediction of such a monumental bluff. Much later, the most celebrated defense by the attorneys of the secessionist leaders, during the trial held at the Supreme Court in Madrid throughout the first half of 2019, under the leadership of Xavier Melero on behalf of the former Minister of Interior of the regional government, Quim Forn (76), also pointed to this conjecture, forming part of a far-reaching political simulation that was accompanied by blatant actions of disobedience, all at the service of forcing an agreement with the central government.

This line of thought had, to almost everyone's surprise, near complete success before the Supreme Court, as the magistrates unanimously assumed that the secessionist adventure was forged and developed based on a simulated assumption, in an "artifice" or a "reverie" (sic), without conclusive evidence that the secession proclamation was intended to be actually made effective, with the forced implantation of a new order to replace the old one. Nevertheless, the court severely condemned the secessionist leaders for sedition and embezzlement, and found that the venture had violated the constitution, had sanctioned the misuse of public funds, and had endangered public order.

There are many intelligent people who have bought this curious story that implies, essentially, that two million citizens (more or less), from an advanced and educated European region, were led to pursue a dream for ten long years and that they remain fully convinced that the promised paradise of an independent Catalonian Republic will soon materialise. I suspect that it did not work that way, although I respect the task of contrasting and balancing evidence to elaborate a well-founded argumentation to sustain the sanctions that the Supreme Court finally dictated.

I suspect that not only because it seems rather improbable that an improvised and obvious bluff could be sustained for so long, keeping your clients firmly convinced that you are fully serious, but also because with a tight and immovable bluff you can win the hand and also the game. This applies to poker as much as it does to the political game.

Whenever there is a debate on this matter with people who have bought into this story of an obvious and easily detectable deception, it is useful to resort to stories to try to counter this vision. The first is a public and very well known one. The second is personal.

Firstly, during the tense weeks in October 2017 that culminated in the official (but failed) proclamation of independence for Catalonia, at the autonomous parliament, the bank branches of villages situated in the vicinity of the dividing line between Catalonia and neighboring Spanish regions including Aragon and Valencia, had to set up afternoon and weekend office hours, to cater for the large influx of Catalan customers eager to open accounts and carry out urgent deposit transfers. Images of those long lines appeared, for several days, on television newscasts from Fraga, Vinarós, Binéfar, Calaceite, Benicarló, Benabarre and other places. The press provided coverage of citizens trying to transfer deposits to accounts in Valencia, Madrid, Zaragoza, Castellón, Almería, Jaén, Badajoz and other Spanish cities, as well as trying to make requests to transfer capital to financial entities outside Catalonia. According to the Central Bank of Spain this leakage of personal deposits from Catalonia amounted to a total of more than 31.4 billion Euros[2]. Notably, this figure is quite close to what the rescue of the Spanish banks ended up costing during the financial crash (2008-2012).

This rush to find a safe haven for private money marries very little, I presume, with the perception of a simulation pushed to the limit by means of an "obvious bluff", with the mere objective of ending up negotiating an arrangement with the Spanish government. It must be stated, however, that I've found people who are still convinced that it was a bluff, but who moved their money quickly and put it safely, outside of Catalonia, "just in case". If nothing else, this is an example of the typical distance between what is said and what is done that makes human behavior so interesting.

The second anecdote is personal.

I spent the sacrosanct day of the "independence referendum" of 1 October 2017 at Solsona, in my family home: a traditionalist and ultra-catholic Catalonia county and one of the iron-clad nuclei of secessionism. I devoted the weekend to staying with my father, in the shifts organised with my brothers, to visit him regularly in his last years as an old and frail senior. Before dawn, from the very early hours of the morning on that Sunday there was a continuous movement of people and vehicles that managed to wake me up. Shortly after nine o'clock a.m., we drove up to the voting point: grandpa was excited to cast his vote. I could not access the brand-new "Multipurpose Room" (for concerts, conferences and social events) that usually functions as the local polling station: all access points were blocked by huge tractors and excavating machines. I got out of the car to enquire with a young man who I could identify as a volunteer. I told him that I needed to get closer as my father was using a wheelchair. He told me to come back after a while because "the computer system had crashed and you won't be able to vote."

We went for a drive through the nearby hills and plains to contemplate, from the vehicle, the autumn forests and the elegantly cultivated fields ready for planting that were opening up through the low clouds. We returned to the polling station after about an hour. We ran into the same impediments again. Another young "volunteer" approached the vehicle and kindly told us that it was still not possible to vote but that he would lead us through an efficient wheelchair pass and that they had arranged a preferential row for disabled and elderly people, for when you could finally vote. He also told us that urgent information was coming to them saying that police contingents could come at any moment. I asked grandpa if he wanted to stay in those conditions. Without hesitating for even a second, he replied that better we were going to return to our trip by car. We did this until one o'clock in the afternoon, when it was time to go to his residence for lunch. During the pleasant drive we stopped at several "rectories": tiny municipal centers with a church, two or three cottages and a sports center, which function as a social club for the farmhouses scattered around and that housed the polling station that day. The same picture awaited us, with huge tractors protecting and blinding access to the polling place. The Police did not come that day in Solsonés, the largest and least populated Catalonian county. It would have taken heavy material and enormous force to overcome the barriers that protected the "right to participate in an illegal vote", in that county at least. Here and there, we merely saw a squad car of the Catalonian police, dubbed the "Mossos", with the occupants chatting placidly as the crucial day passed.

Such sensational logistics and "defensive" displays do not tally easily with the notion of a political challenge based on an obvious "bluff" enacted to sustain only a "simulation", "reverie" or "artifice". In fact, I harbor the suspicion that the magistrates of the Spanish Supreme Court got a major surprise when verifying the degree of violence unleashed by their sentence to the secessionist leaders on October 2019, a sentence which was written with an undeniable touch of interpretive creativity.

The center of Barcelona and other Catalan cities became, for ten long days, a battlefield with display of destruction and vandalism rarely seen before. A violence that reached the point of requiring—for the first time in years—the coordinated action of the regional police, the state police and the national guard, to be able to contain it. This reflected a battle that took place across the whole region that became a cover story for days in media outlets across the world, as did the subsequent repair works for the destruction of infrastructure on roads, railways, streets and also private properties that amounted to an enormous cost (93, 95). It's also worth remembering that when the Spanish prime minister visited wounded agents in hospital in Barcelona, he was heavily surrounded by security guards armed conspicuously with automatic weapons. Rather little of all this seems based on a mere "artifice" or "simulation".[3]

CATSPANISH MELANCHOLY
Temptative Prescriptions

The helplessness and melancholy of the CatSpanish citizenry resurface, without remedy, when verifying the inconsistency and weakness of Spain's response to the crisis. The draw resulting from the secessionist push was due, in the first instance, to the sober stamina showed by the unionist segment of Catalonians across a decade of sustained pressure, and a campaign of social intimidation that was designed to break any bond or link with the reviled Spanish nation. During that time, only limited meaningful support was received from Spain, without solidarity links based on a shared will to embark upon a profitable navigation together, within the complex global panorama, and based on an indisputable democratic solidity, and the confidence sustained by the capacity to create attractive scenarios of shared progress for the whole country.

This lack of self-esteem and security on the part of contemporary Spain is detectable in many areas. The astonishing facility to lose track of "the narrative" and "the story" during practically the entire secessionist crisis, in many of the most prominent forums of the world, openly betrays this (20). Diplomats and members of the Spanish intelligentsia rarely succeed in using the tone to show the required consistency from an important pillar of a united Europe.

Spain engages in endless domestic battles, inflamed and obfuscated by the noise of minor internal discrepancies, and tends to neglect the flanks of external pressure and influence (20). That is an ancient vice, although almost fifty years of uninterrupted democratic conviviality and sensational economic and social progress should have been enough to correct the old propensities for bitterness and sectarian factionalism.

There will always be domestic litigations, of course. The way out lies in not turning them into a reason for unending obsession or paralysing self-absorption. A survey carried out by CEO, the official Catalonian Surveys Agency, throughout all of Spain, involving in-person interviews that reached 3,600 citizens from all Spanish autonomous communities at the end of 2019, illustrated the vast panorama of discrepancies that exist about what is usually called the "territorial debate". See, as an example, the differences that appear in Figures 11.1 and 11.2.

There is a notable radical discordance here, as the Catalonians that were surveyed think that Madrid, Andalusia, Extremadura and the Basque Country receive an excess of good treatment from the central government, in that order. The rest of the Spanish citizenry believe that those who receive privileged treatment are Catalonia, the Basque Country and Madrid, also in that order. With such different perceptions and views there is an unending breeding ground for chronic disagreements.

In this survey, respondents were also asked to indicate the degree of sympathy they felt for their fellow co-nationals from other regions. They had to answer to what extent they liked the individuals of the different autonomous communities, on a scale of zero to ten, where zero was equivalent to "*I really dislike them*" to ten "*I like them very well*". When Catalonians were asked to what extent they sympathize with fellow citizens from the rest of Spain, the average score they gave them was 6.8. In contrast, the score of these fellow citizens for Catalonians was 5.6. This expression of relatively less sympathy for Catalonians appeared in all Spanish regions, without exception. This has been the case for decades, when such surveys

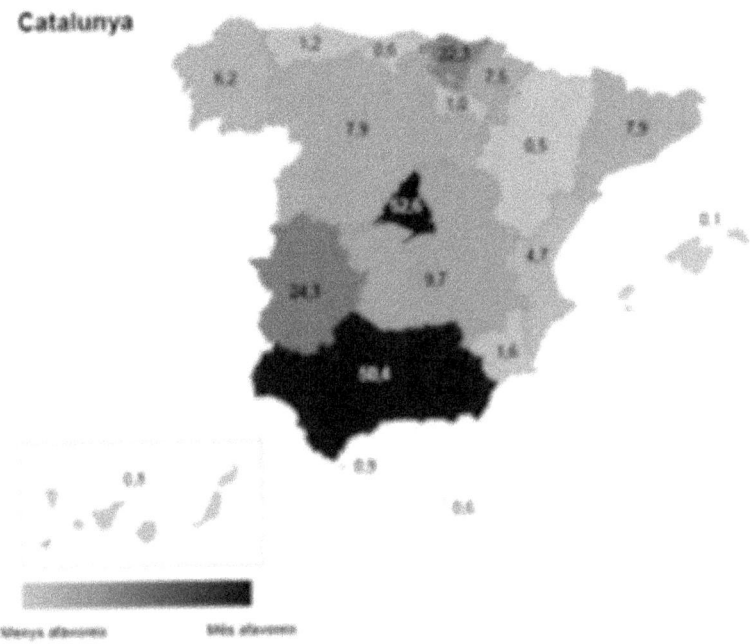

Figure 11.1 Responses to the question "What region do you think is the more privileged by the central State?" The percentages which appear inside these region's maps indicate the total scores obtained for being perceived as a privileged community. Opinions of Catalonian citizenry. Source: http://ceo.gencat.cat/ca/estudis/registre-estudis-dopinio/estudis-de-la-generalitat/detall/index.html?id=7368

are carried out by the CIS—the official Spanish statistical agency—as Catalonians always sit in last place at the gradations of sympathy among the rest of the Spanish citizenry.

If instead of total average scores, other kind of proportions are used, such as 'what percentage of Catalonians do Spaniards dislike?', and 'what percentage of Spaniards do Catalonians dislike?' (with a score of four or less considered to denote 'dislike'), Catalonians are not appreciated by a considerable proportion of their fellow Spaniards. Overall, the bulk of Spaniards who show dislike for Catalonians is 26.1 percent. In Castilia, Cantabria and Asturias, this rejection reaches one third of the population. In the Basque Country

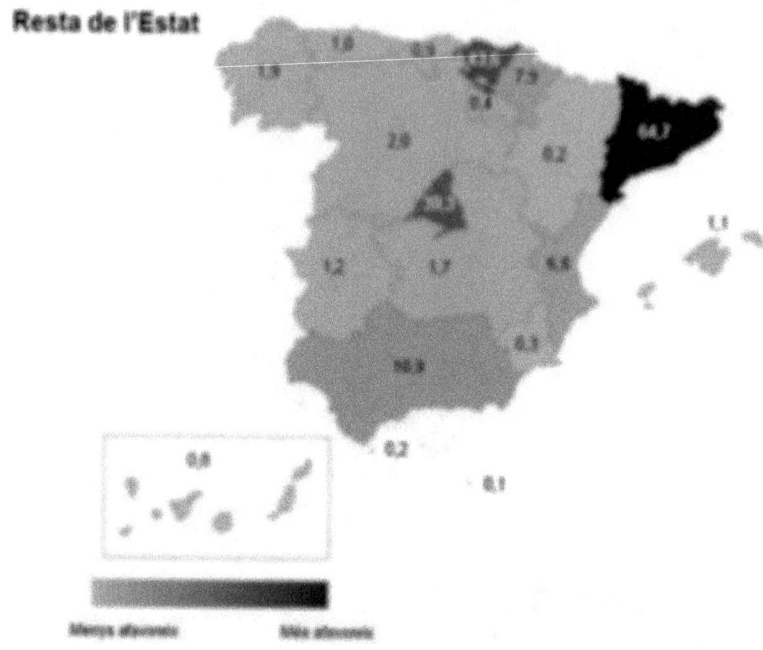

Figure 11.2 Opinions of the rest of Spanish citizens surveyed. The scale of intensities goes from "less privileged" to "more privileged". *Source*: http://ceo.gencat.cat/ca/estudis/registre-estudis-dopinio/estudis-de-la-generalitat/detall/index.html?id=7368

it drops to only 9 percent. The total percentage of Catalonians who dislike Spaniards is low, at 10.2 percent. This antipathy is higher, however, in the case of Madrid: 19 percent of Catalonians express displeasure towards them, although Madrid citizens manifest even greater antipathy towards Catalonians, reaching 28 percent. When the measure is taken to the extreme of antipathy or aversion: '*I really dislike Catalonians*' (a zero, on the scale zero to ten), a similar differential pattern emerges: 9.6 percent of Spaniards express that degree of notorious aversion for Catalonians, while only 1.3 percent of Catalonians say they feel the same about Spaniards (14)

Overall, therefore, the majority of Catalonians feel some sympathy for Spaniards and the majority of Spaniards also express it for

Catalonians, because the average scores exceed 5. It is, however, a very tiny sympathetic score, but it allows respondents to appear as "a good guy" before the pollsters, which seems to be the majority feeling. But 26.1 percent of Spaniards have no problem at all confessing a clear dislike for Catalonians (less than four on the zero to ten scale). And the same happens to 10.2 percent of Catalonians when it comes to Spaniards. With the accentuated antipathy criterion, there are 9.6 percent of Spaniards who feel aversion for Catalonians (zero, on the zero to ten scale), although only 1.3 percent of Catalonians profess to have that same feeling of aversion towards Spaniards.

These figures must be taken with a degree of skepticism, however, because the bulk of surveyed citizens only reached acceptable numbers in Catalonia, Madrid and Valencia. In the rest of regions, the number of surveys collected was too small to draw meaningful conclusions. In any case, a clear finding is that Catalonians are situated in last place in terms of the levels of inter-regional sympathy throughout the rest of Spain. This is one more ingredient to add to the cocktail that nourishes *CatSpanish* melancholy. It seems that the splendid Spanish high speed train network, the INSERSO travel campaigns (promoting cheap holidays for Spanish Seniors everywhere), the Catalan rumba and other types of musical fusion, the region's avant-garde gastronomy, including the adoption of Catalonian "tomato bread" by many Spanish restaurants, and the global influence of the region's football teams, have contributed very little, apparently, to banish or mitigate old apprehensions.

However, there remains precious and still relatively unexplored opportunities for a possible prescription for an "affective" approach to these relationhsips, which has been often pointed out: a prominent Catalonian figure is needed at the top of the Spanish government. In the five decades of a very fruitful and convivial democratic Spain, since the end of the last dictatorship, there has been not a single Catalonian politician commanding the whole country, with only Andalusians, Galicians and Castilians taking the top job, with Madrid, more recently monopolising the top podium. There have been figures of great relevance and influence (e.g. Narcís Serra,

Ernest Lluch, Josep Piqué, and Josep Borrell, among others), but none in the prime minister's office. A strong Catalonian leadership figure could be in order now, and it should be an individual coming with a dual *CatSpanish* identity.

Albert Rivera had this opportunity within his reach, but he blatantly failed. Inés Arrimadas may face the same fate, as she has only had the chance to lead during an almost total collapse of liberal centrism in Spain. So, a potential *CatSpanish* figure for Moncloa Palace will have to spring from the rich variety of mixed sensitivities that grow, incessantly, in the favourable climate of the bourgeois neighbourhoods of downtown Barcelona or from elsewhere in the *CatSpanish* territories. Combining a leadership of this nature with renewed constitutional rules for Spain based on some form of creative federalism, so as to facilitate the multiple set of non-exclusive patriotisms which are now fashionable among political scientists (22, 25, 42, 48, 53, 67, 68, 79, 80, 84, 87, 97, 110, 111), perhaps will provide a viable plan for another thirty or forty years of convivial tranquillity across Spain. It may be that, after all, what Spain really needs is a whole century of progress and amiable coexistence, without major interruptions.

With Catalonia's irreducible secessionists there is no other way than to carry on with them with patience and temperance. These fundamentalists are, of course, another inexhaustible source of melancholy for *CatSpanish* citizens, because there are many of them, numbering between 20 percent and 25 percent of Catalonia's population and they are present in all places, professions and trades. But there is no other formula than stoic patience and vigilant care to deny them exclusive access to the levers of power in the autonomous region, where they easily run wild. It can be said that they are people who prefer, in all circumstances, "a tiny house" (i.e. their region) to a "spacious, open and well-aired home" (i.e. the whole of Spain). When they are reminded that perhaps they were the first to be dubbed "Spaniards" by their Occitan and Provençal relatives, with that word ("*Español*") utterly foreign to the Castilian language, to designate their trans-Pyrenean comrades (2), they do not flinch.

But Catalonian citizens and the rest of the Spanish citizenry have already travelled many centuries together. There is no reason to think that the journey cannot continue on a fruitful course. This itinerary has presented difficulties, obstacles and pitfalls most certainly, but also many reasons for hope and optimism for the citizenry and for the generations to come.

EPILOGUE

"We are trilinguals: we speak Spanish, CatSpanish and only a few, Catalan language"

Quim Monzó, *La Vanguardia-Cultura*, 3-6-2018[1]

Before closing this journey through politically fragmented Catalonia, it is necessary to detail why I have baptised the majority cohort of the region's citizenry with the mixed contraction "*CatSpanish*". I have tried to promote this hybrid label for 65 percent of Catalonian citizens who self-identify, either privately or openly, and to a greater or lesser degree, with at least some elements of the Spanish character, traditions and culture. I do not pretend to replace the traditional name for the Catalonian citizenry (i.e. "*Catalans*"), of course, but only add another label to describe a substantial part of the citizens living in the north-eastern corner of the Iberian peninsula, with the rather naive pretension that it might acquire, perhaps, a positive connotation. In any event, I have used it as a convenient tool to better disclose the masked reality of the dual national identity that can be found in the region.

Such a term *as CatSpanish,* which is an English version of "*Catañoles*" or "*Catanyols*" (the Spanish and Catalan words respectively) was coined decades ago, in fact, and it must be said that it was disseminated widely, partly as illustrated by a quote from one of the more popular Catalan writers (Quim Monzó) at the start of this epilogue. It is typically used to characterise a way of speaking Catalan language that carries a profuse and deep influence from Spanish language. Today, the *CatSpanish* (*Catanyol*) variant is ever-present in Catalan life, and is widely heard and used.

It is necessary to point out, nevertheless, that this venture starts with little hope. First, because within the punctilious and sensitive area of language signalling, *Catanyol (CatSpanish)* already carries a stigma with some contemptuous undertones, because purists always equate foreign influence to toxic contamination, at least when it comes to language. This is why they adorn this majoritarian modality of Catalan-speaking with the attributes of a vulgar and abhorrent *"patois"*. And secondly, because a nickname is much more likely to end up carrying a negative connotation than a positive one when there is fierce competition between neighbours' linguistic practices, and a bulk of findings from the psychology of social prejudice points in that direction (37, 47, 85, 98).

In any case, since a negative valence is already carried by the term *"Catalan"* (see pages 109–111), perhaps a viable gap opens up to devise better prospects. In this endeavour, advertising professionals should be the main guides. Imagine the following "experiment" of social influence: if one of the world's leading footwear brands were to name one of its coolest models *"catañolas"*, recognizing the inspiration derived from local espadrilles—a light shoe with a rich and well-documented tradition in Catalonia—the latent tension in the region could be at least partly resolved. Little more would be needed, I would argue. The ingredients of pride and prestige of wearing a pair of *"catañolas"* would be transferred to the word, and from the word, most likely, to the social identifier. This could be a path to achieve the goal that a coalesced signal—an idiomatic hybrid beacon of sorts—could be adopted, as a prestigious "brand" by people around the world. In other words, this could transmute the *"CatSpanish"* marker into something equivalent to

"African-American" or "Asian-American" in the USA, to successfully overcome the degrading ethnicist or racist overtones of previous idiomatic markers (97, 98).

That is why I deviated during some passages of this essay towards gossip regarding political and other "celebrities" from a variety of backgrounds. While the subject has led us through complex and detailed analysis of statistics to describe the various features of this tense confrontation, I have tried to maintain a somewhat casual tone throughout to enable an informal tone and discussion. In daily discussions, to count on a widely accepted epithet with an affable connotation would serve the region well, presumably, because there are already so many negative and derogatory names. It could even happen that the pathways for a resolution to the current Catalonian crises, within a renovated Spanish political context, would need to be sustained by the firm support of a majority of the *CatSpanish* citizenry.

I suspect, moreover, that progress at the formal "negotiation tables" that Gabriel Rufián—as representative of the leading secessionist ERC party—imposed on the ruling PSOE, to try to find a way to get past the entrenched Catalonian litigation, will require the consent of the *CatSpanish* world. Without that, it will be difficult or impossible for any proposal that emerges to move beyond the stage of ephemeral or empty gestures. A first official meeting of which was held at the Moncloa Palace, Madrid, on 26 February 2020, convened by both the central and regional governments but served only to establish a possible calendar of future meetings and to provide a media photo-opp. As a prelude to this gathering, a range of top ministers from Madrid, Andalusia and the Canary Islands were seated in front of the usual secessionist spokespersons. A prominent *CatSpanish* representative, Salvador Illa, Minister of Health of the central government, a seasoned social democrat without a clear alignment on the issue of secession, was also present[2]. But *CatSpanish* unionists were absent and, apparently, they were not even expected to attend. In short, this was a bad start. Anyone who watches Catalan politics would be unsurprised at such antics, which might have partly been intended to keep the public entertained while also maintaining at least a semblance of ongoing dialogue. In any event, if any approach would allow us to advance on the path towards convivial harmony in Catalonia, they would be very welcome.

In any case, despite the typical volatility and emotive nature of much of what I have discussed throughout this journey, this essay has sought to provide a useful and rigorous account of the many essential features of the politically divided and socially fractured region of Catalonia.

POSTSCRIPT

This essay was almost ready for print when the outbreak of coronavirus stopped life across most of the world, when even the Catalonian secession litigations went into an abrupt and complete halt. They disappeared from the political stage, displaced by the urgency and ferocity of the pandemic. Spain was among the worst affected countries in Europe, with some of the highest rates of infection over the first months of the outbreak. The Madrid region and Catalonia were the most badly affected areas in the country. Spain also endured one of the longest and more restrictive lockdowns in the whole continent. Main political struggles during the first months of the pandemic revolved around the management of pandemic-related issues and the subsequent economic downturn, while previous disagreements and confrontations essentially disappeared during the strange spring and summer of 2020.

It was only a transient illusion, of course, particularly on the issue of the Catalonian political fracture. A CEO survey on the perceived impact of the pandemic[1] provided a good portrait of the ongoing social division, which was carried out at the peak of the viral outbreak and reached 14,715 citizens aged 16 years and older. An overwhelming majority of supporters of the secessionist parties unconditionally approved of the regional government management of the health emergency, while similar proportions of supporters of the non-secessionist parties strongly disapproved of it. Figure P.1 shows the clear division of opinion obtained by differentiating Catalonian citizenship by the national identity groupings to which I have often referred throughout this essay. Those who self-identify as *"only Catalan"* or *"more Catalan than Spanish"* wilfully supported the (secessionist) regional government's measures during the health emergency, whereas those who self-identified either *"As Catalan as Spanish"*, *"more Spanish than Catalan"* or *"only Spanish"* strongly opposed them.

These proportions go into reverse, albeit with a slightly reduced weight, when judging the policies applied by the Spanish government during the onset of the pandemic. Hence, feelings of national

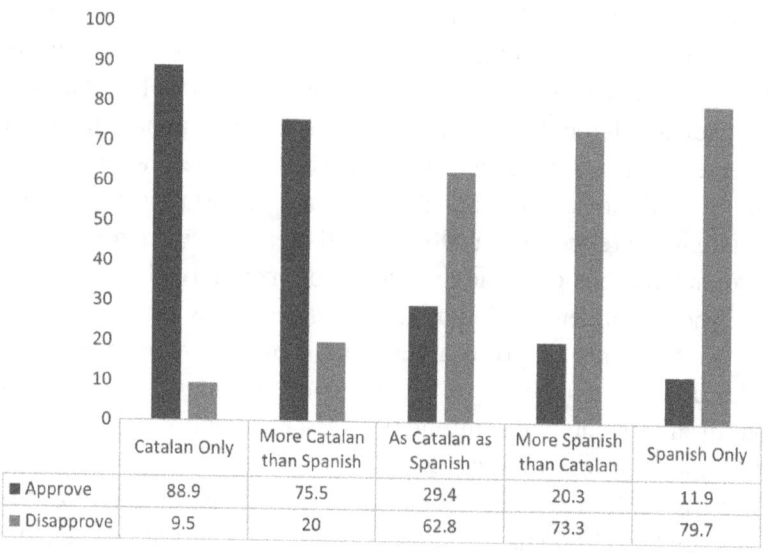

Figure P.1 Perceptions about the efficacy of the Catalonian government during the Covid-19 outbreak, with respondents grouped by feelings of national identity. Based on the aforementioned CEO-Survey (p. 119), 'Approve' expresses support for how "The Regional Government is solving or knows how to deal with the pandemic", while 'Disapprove' denotes how "The Regional Government does not know how to deal with the epidemic". (N=14.715). Modified from Castro C and Aragó L "El "procès" alcanza a la Covid-19", La Vanguardia, 10-5-2020.

identity and factionalism regarding the issue of secession were the main vectors to explain the differential alignment of the Catalonian citizens when judging the performance of the regional government during the hardest part of the fight against Covid-19[2]. Regarding perceptions of the central government's policies during the crisis as it unfolded, it seems that political ideology had as much relevance as feelings of national identity did.

So, despite the difficult and paralysing months that it took to get to grips with the first wave of the catastrophic pandemic and the dire prospects of the subsequent economic crash, the deep fracture in Catalonia on the issue of secession continued alive and mostly untouched.

This is not surprising at all, since the division within the Catalonian citizenry is so profound and ingrained that it has reached the point of neatly separating those affirming from those negating the existence of such a division. The frontier separating these radically divergent opinions ran (as of late 2019) across the same breaking line of secessionists vs unionists. As Figure P.2 shows, the majority of Catalonian citizens (57 per cent) acknowledged that Catalonia was divided in two halves, but such opinion was clearly concentrated among supporters of the unionist parties, while among secessionist party supporters there was a strong conviction that Catalonia remained socially and politically united[3].

A study from survey data, from mid-2018 (89), distinguished the prevalent mood and emotional profiles among representative segments of the unionist and secessionist citizenry. Despite the blatantly unsuccessful climax of the recent bid for secession, at the time of that survey, secessionists felt much less tired and confused than unionists. They referred also to being much less fearful and more hopeful about the political and economic future. These distinctive feelings and disparate beliefs about future difficulties were associated with a cognitive distortion that was noticeable only among secessionists, about the real magnitude of their political force.

I do not know if this has substantially changed since the catastrophe of the pandemic, although results from Figure P.1 suggests that

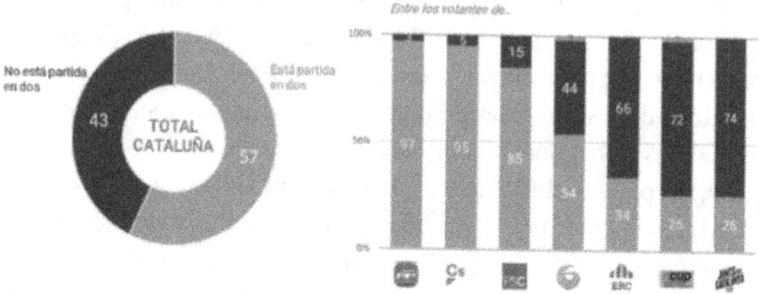

Figure P.2 Opinions regarding the Catalonian division (September 2019).
*Question: Do you think that Catalonia is divided in two halves? Left: Total results expressed in percentatges. Right. Distribution across the main parties. PP: Popular Party (conservatives); C's: Ciudadanos (liberals) PSC: Socialist party (social democrats); ComunsPodem (left populists); ERC: Esquerra Republicana Catalunya (center-left secessionists); JuntsCAT: Together Catalonia (center-right secessionists); CUP: PopularUnionCatalonia (extreme-left secessionists). "No está partida en dos" ("Not divided"); "Está partida en dos" (Divided); "Entre los votantes de "(Among voters of) *Source*: Metroscopia Survey "Cataluña: balance de situación": Interviews to 1500 Catalonian electors >18 years old, 10-13 Sept, 2019. www.metroscopia.org

this has probably not happened. The dividing line that separates the Catalonian citizenry into two main trenches runs apparently along exactly the same frontier.

In sum, the long-lasting entrenchment between the two main segments of the Catalonian citizenry (i.e. unionists and secessionists) will probably continue along similar lines due to the following reasons:

1. All surveys predict that secessionist parties will top the polls at the next regional elections (planned for 14 February 2021), with combined support above 40 per cent for the main pro-secession forces. (This was fully confirmed by the results of these elections). See Postscript II for details.
2. Catalonian secessionist parties are currently indispensable for sustaining the fragile left-wing ruling government in Madrid, putting them in an undeniable position of power.

3. With the secessionists ruling the autonomous administration in Catalonia, which is likely to remain in place in the short-to-medium term, comes the guarantee of commanding and subsidising the main media platforms (which includes TV, radio, and newspapers) and networks that nourish something of an echo-chamber of pro-secessionist opinion.
4. It also warrants the unchanged continuation of the educational system in schools that cultivates and assures the stagnation of social strata within the Catalonian citizenry.
5. The post-Brexit period raises questions about the future constitutional status of Scotland and Northern Ireland, and thus creates opportunities for secessionists to find allies in the European context.
6. Looking through a wider lens, successive regional governments have worked hard to create a network of sympathisers and supporters of the Catalonian secessionist movement among international media and in many influential academic and other circles, across Europe and North America especially.
7. Although major industrial firms and financial corporations have firmly opposed secession during the high-point of the confrontation, there is also a disseminated, important and creative network of enterprises, in many areas, that actively support secession.
8. The most influential trademark of Catalonia around the whole world—Barça F.C.—has been under the heavy influence of secessionist circles (with varying intensities depending on the successive club boards), over the last 15 years. All forecasts suggest that this trend will continue unabated. (A new Presidency was elected at Barça FC, on 7th March 2021, securing the government of the soccer club for secessionists.)
9. A good proportion of important employers, university governments, professional colleges, school boards and the boards of a range of other institutions across the arts, commerce, finance and sport are also under the influence of secessionist circles.

10. Many local celebrities from across the arts and culture, as well as within leading sports and leisure activities, are also under the strong influence of secessionist forces.

So all the necessary conditions for a continuation of the deep social fracture among the Catalonian citizenry that I have described here remain present, despite the blatant failure of the secessionist venture. In fact, the subsequent imprisonment and exile of prominent secessionist leaders, and the trials and sentences[4] by the Supreme Spanish Court that followed, were effectively used, with plenty of half-truths and obvious falsehoods, as propaganda to sustain the fervour and commitment within the secessionist movement.

The unionist field returned, for its part, to the sober and mostly subdued resistance that has characterised it over more than the past decade. In reality, the unionist side can anticipate a further extended period of stoic resistance, while awaiting the intervention of a reinvigorated central government, which at the time of writing continues to feel like a rather distant prospect.

Sant Cugat del Vallès (Barcelona), October 2020.

POSTSCRIPT II

THE 2021 ST VALENTINE'S DAY CATELECTIONS

In mid-January 2021, the regional elections that were scheduled to take place in Catalonia on 14 February 2021 were postponed due to the caution of the regional government—a decision that was subsequentlly anulled by the Catalonian High Court. The elections finally took place on a grey and rainy St Valentine's day in the midst of the pandemic and an economic downturn that was gathering pace. In such circumstances, it might have been expected that practical matters would be foremost in the minds of the Catalonian electorate. However, the deep social fractures that have been created by the secessionist bid and the wounds dating from October 2017 persist. This was when an unlawful referendum for independence and a failed proclamation of secession were followed by a trial at the Spanish Supreme Court in 2019, which saw nine secessionist leaders sentenced to terms in prison.

The backdrop of this election was very different from the last one that took place just over three years ago, in late December 2017, while the region's Home Rule powers were temporarily suspended by the Spanish Parliament. At that time, the elections were defined by the rancorous dispute over Catalan independence between secessionist and unionist segments of the Catalonian citizenry. Fast-forward to 2021, it was the coronavirus pandemic which set the scene—with polling station staff decked out in full personal protective equipment to enable those who had tested positive for the virus to vote (Figure P.3). However, politically, the results were very similar.

Once again the deep political and emotional divide regarding the prospect of Catalan independence dominated the election. The Catalan judicial authorities released the nine jailed secessionist leaders on day-release to allow them to campaign. The separatist parties increased their slender majority of seats in the 135-seat Catalan parliament by four, to 74, but the final turnout was just over 53 percent, the lowest in modern times (down from 79.1 percent at the last election in 2017, and representing only 27.1 percent of the electorate (see Figure P.4). Arguably, people stayed away from the polls in

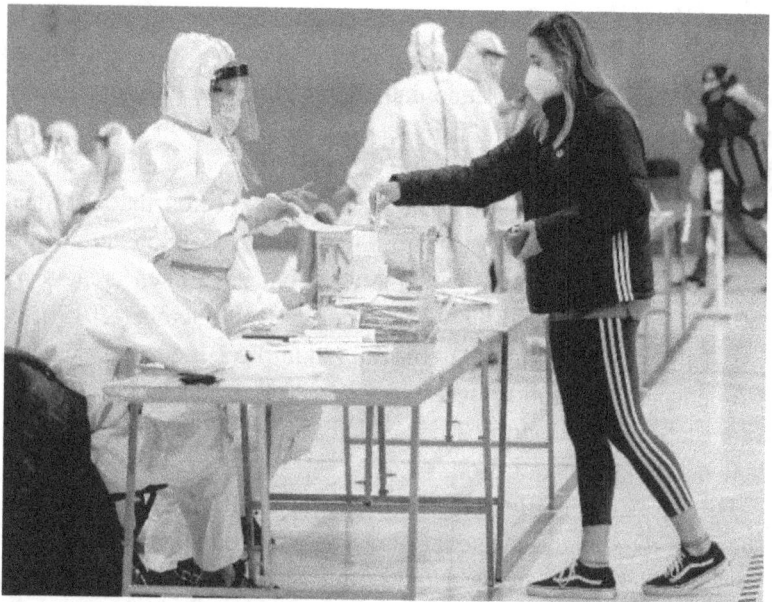

Figure P.3 Voting at Catalan elections, Barcelona downtown, 14th-Feb.-2021.
Source: https://www.elconfidencial.com/espana/cataluna/elecciones-catalanas/2021-02-15/

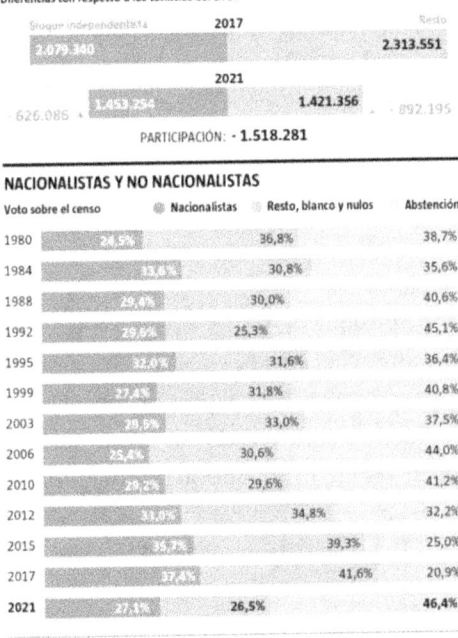

Figure P.4 Turnout evolution and main results on Catalan elections 1980-2021. *Source*: from Castro C., La Vanguardia, 16-Feb-2021. https://www.lavanguardia.com/politica/20210216/6249813/mensaje-silencio.html. Above: Turnout evolution of regional elections 1980-2021; Below: General results (votes) comparing secessionists vs. unionists parties in 2017 vs. 2021 elections and the evolution of the same comparisons (% votes), for these political segments 1980-2021. Before 2010, the secessionist parties identified themselves as nationalists and secession from Spain was not on their agenda. Nacionalistas: secessionists; No-Nacionalistas: unionists; Voto sobre el censo (% total electoral votes), Nacionalistas: Secessionist votes; Resto: Unionist votes; Abstención: Abstentions.

record numbers partly due to the pandemic, but a general political disaffection also played a role.

Thus, these results confirmed once again the persistence of an almost perfect division between unionists and secessionists (roughly 49 vs. 51 percent, respectively) which contrasts with similar—but reversed—proportions in previous elections, with much higher turnouts. Figure P.4 also shows that the big drop in participation affected both camps, though not equally, with the seccessionist parties losing 625,000 votes, and the unionist parties suffering a much higher hemorrhage of votes, with loses approaching 900,000 votes.

The secessionist vote was split among four parties with widely differing electoral strategies. For instance, centre-left ERC (Esquerra Republicana de Catalunya/Republican Left of Catalonia) actively supports the PSOE-Podemos government in Madrid and accepts a "gradualist" path to secession via negotiations on any future referendum. Meanwhile, JxCat and CUP want to proclaim and enact independence unilaterally. The main secessionist forces, with the centre-right JxCAT alliance (of the pro-independence leader Carles Puigdemont) and the ERC party comfortably dominated their fields, achieving a near tie, with the latter edging a narrow victory by a single seat, reversing what had become their traditional order. This has been interpreted by some as a sign of the potential decrease of influence of Puigdemont in both Catalonian and Spanish politics, since he has been based in Waterloo in Belgium and at the EU Parliament (see p. 25).

In fact, PSC,[1] the Catalan branch of Spain's Socialist Party (PSOE), won the election, collecting more votes than any other party, even though it only took 23 percent of the popular vote (Figure P.5). This translates into 33 seats in the regional parliament, the same number as ERC, who will now probably lead the secessionist front and the government with 21 percent of the popular vote. The ERC leader, Oriol Junqueras, continues in prison, having been sentenced for sedition and embezzlement. He was the Vice-president of the Catalonian Government when the referendum for independence was organised and secession proclaimed at 2017. He has been

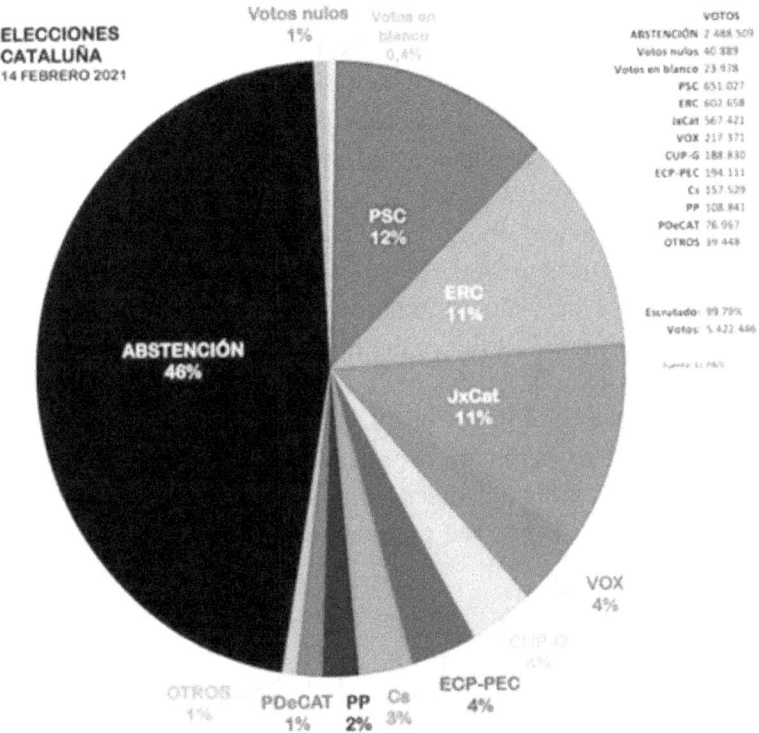

Figure P.5 Results of Catalan elections, 14 February 2021, represented as percentages of overall electorate. *Note*s: PSC (unionist), Catalonian branch of Spanish PSOE; ERC (secessionist), center-left; JxCAT (secessionist), center-right; VOX (unionist), extreme right; CUP-G (secessionist), extreme-left; ECP-PEC (unionist), left-populists, Catalonian branch of Spanish PODEMOS; Cs-CITIZENS (unionist), liberal centrists; PP (unionist) Spanish Conservative Party; PdeCAT (secessionist) centrists. *Source*: Elaborated by JM Oller from official results published in El País (https://elpais.com/)

indicted as unable to run for public office after leaving jail, when the (unofficially announced) pardons by the Spanish Government are expected to arrive. Junqueras' deputy-leader, Pere Aragonés, is the frontrunner to become Catalonia's next President. He immediately adressed a message to European authorities saying *"the results are clear: we, the pro-independence parties have a majority, we have reached more than 50 percent of the popular vote. The Catalan people have spoken, the time has come to negotiate a referendum of self-determination. Please get involved".*

But everybody knows that these results merely confirmed what is essentially an entrenched tie between the secessionists and unionists forces, and that the scant majority of secessionist seats in the regional parliament comes from an old electoral law that grossly over-represents inland counties and grossly under-represents the much more populated coastal areas of the region (see maps at Figs. 1.4, 1.5, 1.6).

The bulk of the unionist vote this time went, to Mr. Salvador Illa, the Minister of Health in the Spanish Government during the pandemic, who only left his Madrid post a few weeks before the elections (see Figure P.6). Polls in the run up to the elections had indicated that his calm and sober demeanor during the coronavirus crisis had been widely appreciated and that he was regarded as a moderate and well-regarded *CatSpanish* politician. Illa was able to

Figure P.6 Mr. Salvador Illa. Minister of Health of the Spanish Government 2020-2021 and winner of the Catalan elections, 14th. February 2021, during a press conference at PSC headquarters, Barcelona. *Source*: (PSC: Partit Socialista de Catalunya)

reverse the big losses that the socialist party (PSC, the Catalonian branch of PSOE) had endured in previous elections. The social democrats thus recovered the lead of the unionist field, overtaking the Ciudadanos Party (*Citizens*: the liberal-centrist party lead by Inés Arrimadas). *Citizens* only won 6 seats this time, plummeting from being the first force in the Catalonian Parliament in the outgoing legislature, with 36 seats, after their surprise victory in 2017. The party suffered a remarkable decline, losing 950.000 votes. The majority of *CatSpanish* citizenry thus returned to their traditional left-wing leanings and systematic abstentionism at Catalan regional elections. Notably, the "differential abstention rate" (between general and regional elections), as is typically named by political scientists, had been almost anulled at the last regional elections.

A big proportion of the *CatSpanish* citizenry were apparently ruminating on the following puzzle: "*our people—the coalition between social democrats and left populists, PSOE+Podemos—now lead the Madrid Government and they had promised to fix the Catalonian conflict: better to stay at home and avoid contagion*". In fact, the big drop in the turnout (a full 25 percent lower than at the 2017 election) was particularly concentrated in the suburban cities in the industrial areas surrounding Barcelona and Tarragona, where the drop in turnout approached or surpassed 30 percent (see maps at Figs. 1.4, 1.5, 1.6).

The appearance of VOX, the main far-right Spanish party, at the Catalan Parliament was the major novelty of these elections. Their results clearly damaged both the main Spanish conservative party, the Partido Popular (PP: Popular party) and Ciudadanos, by securing fourth position in the Chamber with 11 seats. The angriest portion of the unionist citizenry migrated from moderate options to the extreme and ultra-nationalistic right-wing postures of VOX. Notably, the rise of Vox is at least partly a direct result of, and a response to, Catalonian secessionism, and the party's erstwhile absence at the Catalan Parliament was an anomaly that these elections corrected. At the same time, the secessionist extreme-left (CUP party) also increased their representation reaching the fifth position in what is a very fragmented Chamber which has seen an augmentation of the more extreme voices in Catalan politics.

In conclusion, the 2021 St Valentine's Day elections left untouched the general landscape described in this essay. A landscape that can be summarised in the following way:

1. *Catalonian society remains divided on the issue of secession from Spain (Fig. 1.3, p. 6):*
   - 45 percent (aprox.) of citizens want to leave Spain;
   - 45 percent (aprox.) of citizens want to remain in Spain;
   - 10 percent (aprox.) of citizens are agnostic on this issue.
2. *Catalonian society is deeply polarised on the issue of independence*[2]*:*
   - Secessionists often repudiate unionists, as unionists do for secessionists;
   - Agnostics are exhausted of living in the midst of a chronic conflict with a continuous flux of propaganda and unsolved tensions—a mood, it should be said, that is often shared on the unionist side.
3. *These divisions and polarisation cut across three main frontiers*:
   - A lingüistic frontier, which is distinguished by the habitual use of Catalan language vs. Spanish language.
   - A familiy-descent origin frontier, with a distinction drawn between native Catalonians (or assimilated) and migrant Spaniards (both long-standing and more recent arrivals), not fully assimilated.[3]
   - A socio-economic/education divide, separating:
     - Middle classes/highly educated segments, which identify mostly with the secessionists camp;
     - Lower socio-economic classes/less educated segments, which identify mostly with the unionist camp.

Hence, Catalonia's divisions runs through a combination of ethnolinguistic and socioeconomic fault lines. Notably, elites and

the more privileged, are also divided, with a secessionist faction that is more connected to the regional administration and a unionist faction with stronger ties to the rest of Spain[4].
4. *The enduring secession bid:*
   - It is clear that the secessionist camp lacked a clear majority within the electorate at the start of the secessionist campaign, and continues to do so.
   - Support for secession is now disproportionately supported by privileged or well-to-do segments of Catalonian society
   - The secessionist push is actively directed by a disloyal regional government that manages substantial budgetary resources and enjoys full autonomy and capacity to act across a range of policy areas, as allowed for under the Spanish Constitution.
   - This situation will likely endure if secessionists continue to command a majority at the regional parliament. By holding on to power, secessionists are afforded preminence and political leverage at all levels within the region, while also leaving the door open to future developments in the international context, for instance regarding independence from the UK for Scotland or Northern Ireland; if these nations were to leave the UK, this could see another voice claiming international suport for the principle of seccession.

The silent, subdued and stoic resistance of the majority of the *CatSpanish* citizenry is likely to continue, as these last elections brought no substantial change to the electoral landscape in Catalonia. The possibilities for a secessionist coalition lead by an ERC-led Catalonian government to enter into serious and fruitful negotiations with the central government in Madrid have increased marginally, since the PSOE-Podemos government has been sustained in part thanks to votes from ERC, among other parties, from other Spanish regions.

Ending the deep divisions within Catalonian society will take time and ultimately, perhaps only through a transversal coalition between unionist and secessionist moderates in the regional parliament which, at the time of writing, appears to be some way off.

Sant Cugat del Vallès (Barcelona), Spain,
17th February 2021.

REFERENCES

1. Alvarez-Gálvez J, Echavarren JM and Coller X (2018) Bound by blood: the ethnic and civic nature of collective identities in the Basque Country, Catalonia and Valencia, *Nations and nationalism*, 24, 2, 412-431.
2. Alvarez Junco J (2001) *Mater Dolorosa: la idea de España en el siglo XIX*, Madrid: Taurus.
3. Amat J (2015) *El llarg procés: cultura i política a la Catalunya contemporània* (1937-2014), Barcelona: Tusquets.
4. Amat (2017) *La conjura de los irresponsables*, Barcelona: Anagrama.
5. Aspachs-Bracons O, Clots-Figueras I and Masella P (2008) The effects of language at school on identity and political outlooks, *European University Institute-Working Papers*, MWP-2008/36.
6. Aspachs Bracons O, Clots-Figueras I, Costa J and Masella P (2008) Compulsory language educational policies and identity formation, *Journal of European Economic Association: Papers and Proceedings*, 6 (2–3), 433–444.
7. Ayén X (2020) Nosotros, charnegos, *La Vanguardia-Cultura*, 9 Enero, p. 48. https://www.lavanguardia.com/cultura/20200119/472964832528/nosotros-charnegos.htm
8. Barceló J (2014) Contextual effects on subjective national identity, *Nations and Nationalism* 20, 4, 701–720.
9. Barrio A and Rodríguez-Teruel J (2017) Reducing the gap between leaders and voters? Elite polarization, outbidding competition, and the rise of secessionism in Catalonia, *Ethnic and Racial Studies* 40, 10), 1776–1794.

10. Barrio A and Field BN (2018) The push for independence in Catalonia, *Nature Human Behavior*, 2, 713-715.
11. Bel G, Cuadras-Morató X and Rodon T (2019) Crisis? What crisis? Economic recovery and support for independence in Catalonia, *Regional Science Policy and Practice*, 11, 5, 833-848.
12. Bertomeus O (2018) ¿Sigue Cataluña siendo "un sol poble"?, *Agenda Pública*, 3, 5.
13. Boylan BM (2015) In pursuit of independence: the political economy of Catalonia's secessionist movement, *Nations and Nationalism*, 21, 761-785.
14. Brew J (2020) Phobia and philia: what Catalans and Spaniards think of one another, *Vilaweb*, 25 January. https://english.vilaweb.cat/noticies/phobia-philia-catalans-spaniards-think-joe-brew/
15. Bycroft C, Fernandez-Rozadilla C, Ruiz-Ponte C, Quintela I, Carracedo A, Donnelly P and Myers S (2019) Patterns of genetic differentiation and the footprints of historical migrations in the Iberian Peninsula, *Nature Communications*, 10, 551. | https://doi.org/10.1038/s41467-018-08272. /1.
16. Calero J y Choi A (2019) *Efectos de la inmersión lingüística sobre el alumnado castellanoparlante en Cataluña*, Madrid: Fundación Europea Sociedad y Educación, http://www.sociedadyeducacion.org/publicaciones
17. Canal J (2015) Historia mínima de Cataluña, Madrid: Turner.
18. Candel F (1964) *Els altres catalans*, Barcelona: Ed 62.
19. Cappellari L and Di Paolo A (2018). Bilingual schooling and earnings: evidence from a language-in-education reform. *Economics of Education Review*, 64, 90-101.
20. Cardenal JP (2020) *La telaraña: la trama exterior del procès*, Barcelona: Ariel.
21. Chen MK and Rohla R (2018) The effect of partisanship and political advertising on close family ties, *Science*, 360, 1020-1024.
22. Christakis NA (2019) *Blueprint: the evolutionary origins of a good society*, New York: Little, Brown Spark.
23. Cichoka A and Cislak A (2020) Nationalism as collective narcissism, *Current Opinion in Behavioral Sciences*, 34, 69-74.
24. Clots-Figueres I and Masella P (2013) Education, language and identity, *The Economic Journal*, 123, F332-F357.
25. Colomer JM (2018) *España: la historia de una frustración*, Barcelona: Anagrama.
26. Coll J, Molina I y Arias-Maldonado M (Eds.) (2018) *Anatomia del procés*, Madrid: Debate

27. Comerford D and Rodríguez Mora JV (2014) *Regions are not countries: a new approach to the border effect*, Edinburgh Research Explorer, https://www.research.ed.ac.uk/portal/en/publications/regions-are-not-countries(5a527ff8-a6c9-4f58-9bc9-f7d8d657080e).html
28. Convivencia Cívica Catalana (2017) *Perfil del profesorado en Cataluña*. http://files.convivenciacivica.org/Perfil per cent20del per cent20profesorado per cent20en per cent20Catalu per centC3 per centB1a.pdf
29. Cornago-Bonal L, Padilla J and Villa-Llera C (2019) From mutual need to growing rift: Catalan nationalism and the Spanish government, *Policy Network*, policynetwork.org/wp-content/uploads/2019/04/Catalan-paper.
30. Costa A (2019) *The bilingual brain: and what it tells us about the science of language*, London: Allan Lane.
31. Crameri K (2014) *Goodbye Spain? The question of independence for Catalonia*, Eastbourne, UK: Sussex Academic Press.
32. Crameri K (2015) Political power and civil counterpower: the complex dynamics of the Catalan independence movement, *Nationalism and Ethnic Politics*, 21, 104-120.
33. Cuadras-Morató X and Rodon T (2018) The dog that didn't bark: on the effect of the Great Recession on the surge of secessionism, *Ethnic and Racial Studies*, 1-20.
34. Cussó R, Garcia L and Grande I (2018) The meaning and limitations of the subjective national identity scale: the case of Spain, *Ethnopolitics*, 17, 165–180.
35. Dalle Mulle E (2018) *The nationalism of the rich: discourses and strategies of separatist parties in Catalonia, Flanders, Northern Italy and Scotland*, London: Routledge.
36. De Nieves A and Diz C (2019) Dual identity?: A methodological critique of the Linz-Moreno question as a statistical proxy of national identity, *Revista Española de Ciencia Política*, 49, 13–41.
37. Dixon J, Levine M, Reicher S and Durrheim K (2012) Beyond prejudice: are negative evaluations the problem and is getting us to like one another more the solution?, *Behavioral and Brain Sciences*, 35, 411-466.
38. Dowling A (2017) *The rise of Catalan independence: Spain's territorial crisis*, London: Routdlege.
39. Elliot JH (2018) *Scots and Catalans: union and disunion*, New Haven: Yale Univ. Press.
40. Esteban J and Ray D (2008) On the salience of ethnic conflict, *American Economic Review*, 98, 5, 2185-2202.
41. Esteban J, Mayoral L and Ray D (2012) Ethnicity and conflicts: theory and facts, *Science*, 336, 858-865.

REFERENCES

42. Fukuyama F (2018) *Identity*, New York: Farrar, Strauss and Giroux.
43. Garcia C (2013) Strategic communication applied to nation building in Spain: the experience of the Catalan Region, *Public Relations Review*, 39, 558-562.
44. Garcia L (2018) *El naufragio: la deconstrucción del sueño independentista*, Barcelona: Planeta.
45. Garvía R and Santana A (2020) The linguistic regime in Catalan schools: some survey results, *European Journal of Language Policy*, 12,1, 85-108.
46. Gillispie R (2020) *Barcelona, the Left and the Independence movement in Catalonia*, London: Routledge.
47. Giner Sorolla R (2012) *Judging passions: moral emotions in persons and groups*, London: Psychology Press.
48. Ginsburg T and Versteeg (2019) From Catalonia to California: secession in constitutional law, *Alabama Law Review*, 70, 923-985.
49. Golec de Zavala A, Guerra R and Simao C (2017) The relationship between the Brexit vote and individual predictors of prejudice: collective narcissism, right-wing authoritarianism and social dominance orientation, *Frontiers in Psychology*, 8, 2023. doi:10.3389/fpsyg.2017.02023.
50. Griffiths RD, Guillén Alvarez P and Martínez Coma F (2015) Between the sword and the wall: Spain's limited options for Catalan secessionism, *Nations and Nationalism*, 21, 43-61.
51. Guardiola J, Carreras J, Savall J, Messegué J, Antràs P and Sala-Martín X (2014) Give Catalonia its freedom to vote: Our nation deserves the chance to decide on its future, *The Independent*, 10-10-2014.
52. Güell M, Rodríguez Mora JV and Telmer ChI (2015) The informational content of surnames, the evolution of intergenerational mobility and assortative mating, *The Review of Economic Studies*, 82, 2, 693-735.
53. Guibernau M (2007) *The identity of nations*, Cambridge: Polity Press.
54. Guinjoan M and Rodón T (2015) A scrutiny of the Linz-Moreno question, *Publius-The Journal of Federalism*, 46, 128–142.
55. Guntermann E, Blais A, Lago I and Guinjoan M (2018) A study of voting behaviour in an exceptional context: the 2017 Catalan election study, *European Political Science*, doi.org/10.1057/s41304-018-0173-8.
56. Hirschfeld LA (1996) *Race in the making: cognition, culture and child's construction of human kinds*, Cambridge (Mass.): The MIT Press.
57. Hobolt SB, Leeper ThJ and Tilley J (2020) Divided by the vote: affective polarization in the wake of the Brexit referendum, *British Journal of Political Science*, https://doi.org/10.1017/S0007123420000125.

58. Horowitz D (2001) *The deadly ethnic riot*, Berkeley: University of California Press.
59. James, N.A. and Matteson, D.S.(2014) ecp: An R Package for Nonparametric Multiple Change Point Analysis of Multivariate Data. *Journal of Statistical Software* 62 (7), 1–25
60. Jordana J (2019) *Barcelona, Madrid y el Estado: ciudades globales y el pulso por la independencia en Cataluña*, Madrid: Catarata.
61. Lepic M (2017) Limits to territorial nationalization in election support for an independence-aimed regional nationalism in Catalonia, *Political Geography*, 60, 190-202.
62. Linz JJ (1999) Democracia, multinacionalismo y federalismo, *Revista Española de Ciencia Política*, 1, 7–49.
63. López Menacho J (2020) *Yo, charnego: memoria personal de la emigración a Cataluña*, Madrid: Catarata.
64. Luque P (2018) *La secesión en los dominios del lobo*, Madrid: Catarata.
65. Lustick IS, Miodownik D and Eidelson RJ (2004) Secessionism in multicultural states: does sharing power prevent or encourage it? *American Political Science Review*, 98, 209–229.
66. Llaneras K (2017) El apoyo a la independencia tiene razones económicas y de origen social, *El País*. https://politica.elpais.com/politica/2017/09/28/ratio/1506601198_808440.html
67. Maíz R, Lagares N and Pereira M (2018) Catalonia: federalism or secession?, *Open Journal of Political Science*, 8, 495–524.
68. Marí-Klose P (2018) Cataluña deshilachada: procesos de desintegración de una comunidad imaginada, en Coll J, Molina I and Arias-Maldonado M (Eds.) *Anatomía del procés*, Madrid: Debate (pp. 221–246).
69. Marqués T (2019) ´Bestias en forma humana´ o de los daños que causa el discurso peligroso, *Araucaria: Revista Iberoamericana de Filosofía, Política, Humanidades y Relaciones Internacionales*, 21, 42, 553-584.
70. Martí Font JM (2019) *Barcelona y Madrid: decadencia y auge*, Barcelona: EDLibros.
71. Martínez G (2018) *57 días en Piolín*, Madrid: Lengua de trapo.
72. Mas Colell A (2019) Un pasaje estrecho, pero pasaje al fin, *El País: Opinión-Tribuna*, 17-12-2019. https://elpais.com/elpais/2019/12/16/opinion/1576498536_916852.html
73. Mason L (2018) *Uncivil agreement: how politics became our identity*, University Chicago Press.

74. Mason L and Wronski J (2018) One tribe to bind them all: how our social group attachments strengthen partisanship, *Advances in Political Psychology*, 39, Supp 1, 257-277.
75. Maza A, Villaverde J and Hierro M (2019) The 2017 Regional Election in Catalonia: an attempt to understand the pro-independence vote, *Economia Política*, 36, 1-18.
76. Melero X (2019) *El encargo*, Barcelona: Ariel.
77. Miley Th J (2007) Against the thesis of the "civic nation": the case of Catalonia in contemporary Spain, *Nationalism and Ethnic Politics*, 13, 1-37.
78. Miley ThJ (2013) Blocked articulation and nationalist hegemony in Catalonia, *Regional and Federal Studies*, 23, 1, 7-26.
79. Miley Th and Garvía R (2019) Conflict in Catalonia: a sociological approximation, *Genealogy*, 3, 56; doi:10.3390/genealogy3040056.
80. Minder R (2017) *The struggle for Catalonia: rebel politics in Spain*, London: Hurst and Co.
81. Moffett MW (2019) *The human swarm: how our societies arise, thrive and fall*, New York: Basic Books.
82. Morel S (2018) *En el huracán catalán*, Barcelona: Planeta.
83. Moreno L (1988) Identificación dual y autonomía política: los casos de Escocia y Cataluña, *Revista Española de Investigaciones Sociológicas*, 42, 155–174.
84. Moreno C (2020) The Spanish plurinational labyrinth: practical reasons for criticising the nationalist bias of others while ignoring one's own nationalist position, *Genealogy*, 4, 7. doi:10.3390/genealogy4010007.
85. Nesseler C, Gómez-González C and Dietl H (2020) What's in a name?: measuring acces to social activities with a field experiment, *Palgrave Communications*, 5, 160. https://doi.org/10.1057/s41599-019-0372-0.
86. Núñez Seixas XM (2018) *Suspiros de España: historia del nacionalismo español* (1808-2018), Madrid: Crítica.
87. OEC Group (2017) *La Cataluña immune al procés*, SCC, Barcelona, 20th April.
(https://www.societatcivilcatalana.cat/sites/default/files/docs/La-Cataluna-inmune-vf.pdf).
88. Oller JM and Satorra A (2017) Toward an index of political toxicity, *BEIO*, 33, 2, 163–182. http://www.seio.es/BBEIO/BEIOVol33Num2/index.html#86.
89. Oller JM, Satorra A and Tobeña A (2019) Secessionists vs unionists in Catalonia: mood, emotional profiles and beliefs about secession

perspectives in two confronted communities, *Psychology*, 10, 336–357. https://doi.org/10.4236/psych.2019.103024.
90. Oller JM, Satorra A and Tobeña A (2019a) Pathways and legacies of the secessionist push in Catalonia: linguistic frontiers, economic segments and media roles within a divided society, *Policy Network Paper*, October, https://policynetwork.org/publications/papers/pathways-and-legacies-of-the-secessionist-push-in-catalonia/.
91. Oller JM, Satorra A and Tobeña A (2019b) Unveiling pathways for the fissure among secessionists and unionists in Catalonia: identities, family language and media influence, *Palgrave Communications*, 5, 148. doi:10.1057/s41599-019-0357-z.
92. Oller JM, Satorra A and Tobeña A (2020) Privileged rebels: a longitudinal analysis of distinctive economic traits of Catalonian secessionism, *Genealogy*, 4, 19. doi: 10.3390/genealogy40.10019.
93. Olmeda JA (2020) Cataluña en el laberinto del minotauro: un espejo roto en la España fragmentada, *Cuadernos de Pensamiento Político*, 65, 15-28.
94. Ortiz Barquero C (2019) The electoral breakthrough of the radical right in Spain: correlates of electoral support for VOX in Andalusia (2018), *Genealogy*, 3, 72. doi: 10.3390/genealogy3040072.
95. Pretus C, Hamid N and Sheikh H (2019) *Impact of legal punishment of nationalist political leaders on social polarization*, Working Paper, Artis International Research: St Michaels, Maryland, USA.
96. Piketty Th (2019) *Capital and Ideology*, Cambridge (Mass.): Harvard University Press.
97. Putnam RD (2007) E pluribus unum: diversity and community in the twenty-first century, *Scandinavian Political Studies*, 30, 2, 137–174.
98. Quattrociocchi W, Conte R and Lodi E (2011) Opinions manipulation: media, power and gossip, *Advances in Complex Systems*, 14, 567–586.
99. Quattrociocchi W, Caldarelli G and Scala A (2014) Opinion dynamics on interacting networks: media competition and social influence, *Scientific Reports*, 4, 4938.
100. Quiroga A and Molina F (2020) National deadlock: hot nationalism, dual identities and Catalan independence (2008–2019), *Genealogy*, 4, 1, 15. https://doi.org/10.3390/genealogy4010015.
101. Qvortrup M (2014) *Referendums and Ethnic Conflict*, Philadelphia: University of Pennsylvania Press.
102. Robles Lucena C (2019) Los amantes bilingües, *Letra Global*, 15 Marzo (reproducido en *Letra Global 2020*). https://cronicaglobal

.elespanol.com/letra-global/el-dossier/los-amantes-bilinguees_229554_102.html.
103. Rodon T and Guinjoan M (2018) When the context matters: identity, secession and the spatial dimension in Catalonia, *Political Geography*, 63, 75-87.
104. Rodríguez-Díaz R, Blanco-Villegas MJ and Mann F (2017) From surnames to linguistic and genetic diversity: five centuries of internal migrations in Spain, *Journal of Anthropological Sciences*, 95, 249-267.
105. Rodríguez-Pose A and Hardy D (2020) Reversal of economic fortunes: institutions and the changing ascendancy of Barcelona and Madrid as economic hubs, *Growth and Change*, 1-23. DOI: 10.1111/grow.12421.
106. Roeder PhG (2018) *National secession: persuasion and violence in independence campaigns*, Ithaca: Cornell University Press.
107. Romero-Vidal X (2019) Two temperatures for one thermostat: the evolution of policy attitudes and suport for independence in Catalonia 1991-2018, *Nations and Nationalism*, 1-19, https://doi.org/10.1111/nana.12559.
108. Ruiz Jiménez AM (2007) Los instrumentos de medida de las identidades en los estudios del CIS y el Eurobarómetro: problemas de validez de la denominada escala Moreno, *Revista Española de Investigaciones Sociológicas*, 117, 161–182.
109. Rul J (2019) *Nacionalismo catalán y adoctrinamiento escolar*. Ed. Amarante.
110. Schatz RT, Staub E and Lavine H (1999) On the varieties of national attachment: blind versus constructive patriotism, *Political Psychology*, 20, 1, 151-174.
111. Seoane LF, Loredo X, Monteagudo H and Mira J (2019) Is the coexistence of Catalan and Spanish possible in Catalonia? *Palgrave Communications*, 5, 139. doi.org/10.1057/s41599-019-0347-1.
112. Shoemaker E and Stremlau N (2014) Media and conflict: an assessment of evidence, *Progress in Development Studies*, 14, 2, 181–195.
113. Sidanius J, Feshbach S, Levin S and Pratto F (1997) The interface between ethnic and national attachment: ethnic pluralism or ethnic dominance? *The Public Opinion Quarterly*, 61, 1, 1, 102-133.
114. Solé-Morata N, Bertranpetit J, Comas D and Calafell F (2015) Y-chromosome diversity in Catalan surname samples: insights into surname origin and frequency, *European Journal of Human Genetics*, 23, 1549-1557.
115. Sorens J (2005) The cross-sectional determinants of secessionism in advanced democracies, *Comparative Political Studies*, 38, 304-326.

REFERENCES

116. Stella M, Ferrara E and De Domenico M (2018) Bots increase exposure to negative and inflammatory content in online social systems, *PNAS*, 115, 12435-12440. doi: 10.1073/pnas.1803470115.
117. Tarín S (2020) *En el tsunami catalán: una biografía del proceso independentista*, Barcelona. Galaxia Gutenberg.
118. Tobeña A (2017) *La pasión secesionista: psicobiología del independentismo*, Barcelona: EDLibros (English version *"The secessionist passion"*, Madrid: Euromind-Funambulista Ed., 2019).
119. Tobeña A (2017a) Secessionist urges in Catalonia: media indoctrination and social pressure effects, *Psychology*, 8, 77-96.
120. Tobeña A (2018) Entrenched Catalonia: a secessionist venture trapped on an ethnopolitical draw, *Psychology*, 9, 460-471.
121. Tormos R, Muñoz J and Hierro MJ (2014) Endogenous identities? How the independence debate is reshaping Catalans' identity, IBEI Workshop *The Politics of Identity Adoption*, Barcelona. http://www.cuimpb.cat/files/TormosMu
122. Ucelay-da Cal E (2018) *Breve historia del separatismo catalán*, Barcelona: Penguin Random House.
123. Vergés-Gifra J, Serrano I and Serra M (2019) *Un biaix etnicista en la política catalana?: l'efecte desigual del procés*, Informe Càtedra Ferrater-Mora: Universitat de Girona.
124. Vidal P (2012) *El catanyol es cura*, Barcelona: Barcanova.
125. Vilarrubias M (2018) *Por una ley de lenguas: convivencia en el plurilingüismo*, Barcelona: Deusto.
126. Von Babel JJ and Pereira A (2018) The partisan brain: an identity-based model of political belief, *Trends in Cognitive Sciences*, 22, 3, 213-223.
127. Westwood SJ, Iyengar S, Walgrave S, Leonisio R, Miller L and Strijbis O (2018) The tie that divides: cross-national evidence of the primacy of partyism, *European Journal of Political Research*, 57, 333–354.
128. Woolard KA (2016) Singular and plural: ideologies of linguistic authority in 21st century Catalonia. Oxford: Oxford University Press.
129. Zmigrod L, Rentfrow PJ and Robbins TW (2018) Cognitive underpinnings of nationalistic ideology in the context of Brexit, *PNAS*, 115, 19, E4532-E4540.
130. Zuber ChI and Szocsik E (2015) Ethnic outbidding and nested competition: explaining the extremism of ethnonational minority parties in Europe, *European Journal of Political Research*, 54, 784–801.

NOTES

PREFACE

1. I prefer to use the word *"unionists"* for non-secessionist Catalonian citizens, for practical reasons. I am aware that some of these citizens can be uneasy with that denomination because it is commonly used as an insult in Catalonia. But it is also the most frequent denomination, everywhere, for individuals who are in favour of forms political integration: those who express preferences for federal or other kind of alliances within and between states. Typical well-known examples: both democrats and republicans at the United States of America, or those European citizens who promote deepening the existing links within the European Union.

2. https://policynetwork.org/publications/papers/pathways-and-legacies-of-the-secessionist-push-in-catalonia/

SITUATION MAPS

1. Source: EULP2018-Enquesta Usos lingüístics de la població, Institut Estadístic Catalunya; (https:// www.idescat.cat/pub/?id=eulp).

2. PSOE is the main social democratic party in Spain.

3. In Spain the "Supreme Court" is the highest judiciary level. The "Tribunal Constitucional" (High Spanish Court) is the highest instance for both legislative and judiciary litigations, equivalent to the Supreme Court in other Western countries.

4. http://ceo.gencat.cat/ca/barometre/).
5. http://www.cis.es/cis/opencm/ES/11_barometros/index.jsp
6. http://ceo.gencat.cat/ca/barometre/
7. *JxCat: Junts per Catalunya,* centre-right nationalist party; *ERC: Esquerra Republicana de Catalunya*: center-left nationalist party; *CUP: Candidats Unitat Popular:* radical-left nationalist party.
8. https://gesop.net/ca/2019/11/11/resultats-a-catalunya-de-les-eleccions-del-10n/

CATSPANISH CITIZENRY

1. ERC (Esquerra Republicana de Catalunya) is a traditionalist, separatist, centre-left party founded during the tumultuous years of the 2nd Spanish Republic in the 1930s.
2. Hectic political manoeuvers as Spanish politics heads towards a highly polarised regional election at Madrid province (4th. May 2021), are apparently threatening a full and definitive dismantling of *Citizens* party.
3. *"Botifler"* is the preferred Catalan word for *"traitor to the homeland"* and is a gross insult.
4. *"Catañol-Catanyol"* is the mix concoction—from "Catalan" and "Español"—denomination that receives this dialect or *patois* variant of Catalan language.

THE VOID OF THE CENTRAL SPANISH STATE

1. https://elpais.com/elpais/2019/06/10/eps
2. Jordi Pujol was the more prominent leader of contemporary Catalan nationalism and President of Autonomous Government of Catalonian from 1980 to 2003. His party (*CDC: Convergència Democràtica de Catalunya*) has been the dominant force in Catalonia for almost 40 years.
3. http://www.exteriores.gob.es/Portal/en/PoliticaExteriorCooperacion/MarcaEsp/Paginas/inicio.aspx

SECESSIONIST TOP LEADERS

1. The results of the Catalan regional elections of 14th February 2021, gave the forces of Carles Puigdemont only the second place among the

secessionist parties, after ERC (Esquerra Republicana de Catalunya), with a difference of 30,000 votes, and a single seat difference at the regional parliament (see Postscript II, p. 125). Puigdemont had allowed a segregation of moderate secessionists in his party (PdeCAT, centrists), that won 70, 000 votes, at the 2021 election, depriving him of another victory. Puigdemont thus lost the leading position he had comfortably enjoyed from exil in Waterloo, while prominent collaborators and allies from his deposed government continue their jail terms. This has been generally interpreted as a sign of a decrease in influence of Puigdemont in both Catalonian and Spanish polítics. Nonetheless, from his bases in Belgium and at the EU Parliament, Puigdemont remains a significant political force, where he exploits his profile as an "exiled" and "victimized" former-President.

MADRID-BARCELONA COMPETITION

1. https://www.elespanol.com/opinion/20171013/253974992_0.html)
2. Hôtel Matignon: the official residence of the France Prime Minister, in Paris.
3. Moncloa Palace: the official residence of Spanish Prime Minister, in Madrid.

DUAL IDENTITIES

1. "*Charnegos*" is a derogatory name given by Catalonian natives to migrants arrived from the rest of Spain, in a series of waves throughout the 20th century.
2. https://www.idescat.cat/poblacioestrangera/

CANTONALISM AND CAINISM IN SPAIN

1. The rule of Constitutional Article 155 denotes the suspension of home rule and that implicated the suspension of the regional government and the closure of the autonomous parliament, with the central state administration taking control of the region.
2. "*El País*": the main Spanish newspaper, with a moderate left-wing, social-democrat tendency.

3. SER: Sociedad Española de Radiodifusión. The leading broadcasting station in Spain.

LONGITUDINAL PROFILES OF CATALONIAN CITIZENRY

1. This chapter is an adaptation of Oller JM, Satorra A and Tobeña A (2019) Pathways and legacies of the secessionist push in Catalonia: linguistic frontiers, economic segments and media roles within a divided society, *Policy Network Paper*, October, https://policynetwork.org/publications/papers/pathways-and-legacies-of-the-secessionist-push-in-catalonia/, and a summary of the series of research papers referenced here as (89, 90, 91, 92). The Figures and Tables have been redrawn to incorporate data from 2020 Barometers.
2. The ecp is an R package designed to carry out nonparametric multiple change point analysis of multivariate data (59).
3. Until summer 2011 the survey question explicitly asked for "family language", after that for "childhood language in the family". This change resulted in a decrease of percentages of people who answered "both languages" and increases on the Spanish-mother language group, but it did not significantly affect other variables within the surveys immediately before and after that change.
4. EULP2018: Enquesta usos lingüístics de la població, Institut Estadístic Catalunya. https://www.idescat.cat/pub/?id=eulp

IMMERSIVE EDUCATION

1. Several studies show that primary and secondary school teachers are highly politically motivated. The proportion of those whose national identity feeling is *'only Catalan'* is higher (reaching more than 40%), than the corresponding proportion of this category in the overall population (22% at the last CEO survey, but always less than 30%, even at 2014), along with higher rates of voters to pro-secession forces than in the general population (28).

A DANGEROUS DECADE (2010-2020)

1. Some terms of imprisonment and exile that continue to the time of writing.

2. https://www.lavanguardia.com/economia/20180320/441737523012/fuga-depositos-cataluna-independencia.html
3. Tobeña A (2020) Catañoles: Barcelona: Ed Libros (pp. 135-136)

EPILOGUE

1. https://www.lavanguardia.com/cultura/20180603/444025825563/quim-monzo-premi-honor-lletres-catalanes.html.
2. In a last minute surprise, the Catalonian branch of PSOE party anounced that Mr. Salvador Illa would be the candidate for President of Catalonia, at the approaching Regional Election (14th. Feb. 2021). This movement changed the electoral prospects, according to most surveys, since he could be a very strong opponent to the secessionsist candidates due to his recent popularity gained through a sober and calm management of the pandemic crisis.

POSTSCRIPT

1. http://ceo.gencat.cat/ca/estudis/registre-estudis-dopinio/estudis-dopinio-ceo/societat/detall/index.html?id=7588
2. On the eve of US presidential election, 3th. Nov. 2020, a group of leading political scientists published an essay on "*Political sectarianism in America*" (Finkel EJ et al (2020) *Science*, 370, 6516, 533-536), describing the main psychological ingredients (distance, aversion and hate), characterizing the alarming rise of partisanship and social polarization at the US. Such political sectarianism is equivalent to the cainism/factionalism described in this book for the social division created in Catalonia. They reported, in that paper, that Spain was second only, after the US, on the perceived increase of national division since Covid-19 pandemic arrived, according to a *Pew Research* survey which compared citizen's opinions on 14 advanced countries (https://www.pewresearch.org/global/2020/08/27/most-approve-of-national-response-to-Covid-19-in-14-advanced-economies)
3. Several surveys have confirmed the continuation of that entrenched and huge political division along 2020. Even studies issued from official organisms of the regional government of Catalonia, devoted to promote

peace and dialog, have produced findings on the similar vein (Barbet B (2020) Survey on polarisation and coexistence in Catalonia, ICIP-Report-17. http://icip.gencat.cat/web/.content/continguts/publicacions/documents_i_informes/2020/informes_2020-17_cat.pdf). Recent findings from studies directed to discern the degree and persistence of polarization/division on the issue of secession have fully confirmed the entrenchment of Catalonian citizenry in two opposed fronts (Balcells L, Fernández-Albertos J and Kuo A (2021) Secession and social polarization: evidence from Catalonia, *UNU-WIDERWorking Paper* 21, https://doi. org /10. 35188 /UNU -WIDER /2021 /936 -5.; Hierro MJ and Queralt D (2020) The divide over independence: explaining preferences for secession in an advanced open economy, *American Journal of Political Science*, in the press, DOI: 10.1111/ajps.12549)".

4. As of today, more than a year after a seemingly harsh sentence, the condemned secessionist leaders have already enjoyed a variety of semi-open experiences while in detention, and the central government announced in Autumn 2020 that legal procedures were underway to award limited pardons for those concerned.

POSTSCRIPT II

1. PSC: Partit Socialista de Catalunya.
2. Recent and illuminating data on this crucial issue: Balcells L, Fernández-Albertos J and Kuo A (2021) Secession and social polarization: evidence from Catalonia, UNU-WIDER-Working Paper 21, https://doi.org /10.35188/ UNU-WIDER/2021/936-5.
3. Llaneras K (2021) Así se relacionan en Cataluña la renta, el voto, el origen y la independencia, *El País*, 20th Feb., https://elpais.com/politica /2021/02/19/actualidad/1613741557_146092.html
4. Though it must be said that a detailed and systematic analysis of these differences within the Catalonian elites is yet to be undertaken.

ABOUT THE AUTHOR

Adolf Tobeña is Emeritus Professor of Psychiatry at the Autonomous University of Barcelona (UAB). He researches on neurobiology of fearfulness and neuroimage of mental disorders at the Unit of Medical Psychology, School of Medicine, Bellaterra Campus. He is the author of 20 books and 190 papers published in journals of neuroscience, psychiatry and psychology. He was visiting professor at the Institute of Psychiatry (University of London), and at the Universities of Groningen, Tel Aviv, Venice, and Córdoba (Argentina). He has directed radio programs and written columns in Barcelona media on scientific topics. His awards include: City of Barcelona, Science, 1992; Avui, Scientific Journalism, 1991; Serra i Moret, Civic Promotion, 1994; European-Estudio General, Scientific Popularization, 2004; Serra d'Or, Scientific Essay, 2014: His most recent books include: Values, empathy and fairness across social barriers New York: Annals NYAS, Vol. 1167, 2009 (Co-Ed); Píldoras o Freud Madrid: Alianza, 2012; Devotos y descreídos: biología de la religiosidad, Valencia: PUV, 2014; La Pasión Secesionista, Barcelona: EDLibros, 2016; Neurología de la Maldad, Barcelona: Plataforma, 2017; Manipuladores Barcelona: Plataforma, 2019; and Talento desperdiciado Barcelona: EDLibros, 2019.

www.ingramcontent.com/pod-product-compliance
Lightning Source LLC
Chambersburg PA
CBHW052049300426
44117CB00012B/2048